The Soul Shield
The Art of Energetic Defense

Helena Costa

Original Title: *The Soul Shield – The Art of Energetic Defense*
Copyright © 2025, published by Luiz Antonio dos Santos ME.
This book is a non-fiction work that explores practical and conceptual approaches in the field of spiritual protection and energetic self-defense. Through an integrative perspective, the author offers powerful tools rooted in diverse traditions to strengthen personal energy and spiritual resilience.

1st Edition
Production Team
Author: Helena Costa
Editor: Luiz Santos
Cover Design: Studios Booklas / Mira Dallin
Consultant: Kael Morné
Researchers: Tessa Wynne / Nolan Dreer / Indira Samesh
Layout Design: Brevin Core

Publishing and Identification
The Soul Shield – The Art of Energetic Defense
Booklas Publishing, 2025
Categories: Spirituality / Energy Healing / Esoteric Studies
DDC: 133.9 — **CDU:** 133.5

All rights reserved to:
Luiz Antonio dos Santos ME / Booklas Publishing

No part of this book may be reproduced, stored in a retrieval system, or transmitted by any means—electronic, mechanical, photocopying, recording, or otherwise—without the prior and express permission of the copyright holder.

Summary

Systematic Index 5
Prologue 9
Chapter 1 Invisible Forces and Influences 13
Chapter 2 The Power of Intention 20
Chapter 3 Sacred Symbols 26
Chapter 4 Prayer and Christian Faith 33
Chapter 5 Amulets in Islam 38
Chapter 6 Hindu Mantras and Yantras 44
Chapter 7 Ancestral Smudging 50
Chapter 8 Shield Meditation 56
Chapter 9 Ritualistic Baths 62
Chapter 10 Ancestors and Guides 68
Chapter 11 Lunar Rituals 75
Chapter 12 Exu and Guardians 81
Chapter 13 Kabbalah and the Tree of Life 87
Chapter 14 Norse Runes 93
Chapter 15 Protective Feng Shui 99
Chapter 16 Magic Circles 105
Chapter 17 Psychoanalysis of Evil 111
Chapter 18 Reconnective Healing 117
Chapter 19 Light Codes 122
Chapter 20 Comparative Exorcisms 127
Chapter 21 Crystals and Earth Mines 132
Chapter 22 Ayahuasca and Purging 138

Chapter 23 Guardian Angels 144
Chapter 24 Defensive Psychography 150
Chapter 25 Tai Chi and Vital Energy 156
Chapter 26 Symbolic Sacrifices 161
Chapter 27 Spiritual Cyberprotection 167
Chapter 28 Ecology and Planetary Defense 173
Chapter 29 Oaths and Pacts 179
Chapter 30 Integrated Self-Defense System 184
Epilogue 189

Systematic Index

Chapter 1: Invisible Forces and Influences - Addresses the existence and impact of unseen energies and entities across various global traditions and their effect on human life.

Chapter 2: The Power of Intention - Explores how focused will and intention serve as the crucial foundation for effective spiritual protection and energy work.

Chapter 3: Sacred Symbols - Details the use and power of various ancient symbols from diverse cultures as tools for spiritual defense and energetic sealing.

Chapter 4: Prayer and Christian Faith - Discusses the role of prayer, faith, scripture (like Psalm 91), and sacramentals within Christianity as methods for spiritual protection.

Chapter 5: Amulets in Islam - Covers protective practices within Islam, including specific Quranic verses, talismans (ta'wiz), and the significance of divine names.

Chapter 6: Hindu Mantras and Yantras - Explains the protective and aligning power of Hindu mantras (sacred sounds) and yantras (geometric diagrams) as spiritual technologies.

Chapter 7: Ancestral Smudging - Describes the ancient and cross-cultural practice of burning herbs and resins to cleanse spaces and energy fields for protection.

Chapter 8: Shield Meditation - Focuses on techniques involving visualization and meditation to consciously build energetic shields for spiritual defense.

Chapter 9: Ritualistic Baths - Details the preparation and use of baths infused with herbs, salts, and intention for spiritual cleansing, purification, and protection.

Chapter 10: Ancestors and Guides - Explores the importance of honoring and connecting with ancestors and spiritual guides as a source of protection and wisdom.

Chapter 11: Lunar Rituals - Discusses how aligning rituals with the different phases of the moon can amplify intentions for protection, cleansing, or manifestation.

Chapter 12: Exu and Guardians - Addresses the role of Exu and Pomba Gira in Afro-Brazilian traditions as powerful spiritual guardians of crossroads and portals.

Chapter 13: Kabbalah and the Tree of Life - Introduces the Kabbalistic Tree of Life, Hebrew divine names, and sigils as complex methods for spiritual understanding and protection.

Chapter 14: Norse Runes - Explains the use of ancient Norse runes not just as an alphabet, but as living symbols and vibrational keys for protection and magic.

Chapter 15: Protective Feng Shui - Describes how the principles of Feng Shui harmonize energy flow (Qi) in environments, creating spiritually protective spaces.

Chapter 16: Magic Circles - Details the practice of casting magic circles in various traditions to create sacred, energetically sealed spaces for rituals and protection.

Chapter 17: Psychoanalysis of Evil - Connects psychological concepts like the unconscious and shadow work (Jung) to spiritual protection, highlighting self-knowledge as defense.

Chapter 18: Reconnective Healing - Discusses reconnective healing as an energy modality accessing cosmic frequencies to restore the being's original energetic signature for healing and protection.

Chapter 19: Light Codes - Introduces the use of specific numeric sequences and sacred geometry as vibrational codes to activate energy fields and provide protection.

Chapter 20: Comparative Exorcisms - Compares exorcism and deliverance practices across various spiritual traditions as methods for liberating individuals from possessing entities.

Chapter 21: Crystals and Earth Mines - Explores the use of different crystals and stones as tools for grounding, energetic shielding, purification, and defense.

Chapter 22: Ayahuasca and Purging - Discusses the ritualistic use of the sacred Amazonian brew Ayahuasca for deep energetic and spiritual cleansing (purging) as a path to protection.

Chapter 23: Guardian Angels - Covers the cross-cultural belief in guardian angels as designated beings of light offering personal guidance and spiritual protection.

Chapter 24: Defensive Psychography - Explains psychography (spirit writing) as a mediumistic tool used defensively to diagnose spiritual interferences and receive protective guidance.

Chapter 25: Tai Chi and Vital Energy - Describes the practice of Tai Chi Chuan as meditation in motion that cultivates and balances vital energy (Qi) for health and spiritual shielding.

Chapter 26: Symbolic Sacrifices - Explores the concept of sacrifice, from ancient rituals to modern symbolic acts like fasting, as a method of vibrational transmutation and protection.

Chapter 27: Spiritual Cyberprotection - Addresses the need for energetic awareness and protection within digital spaces, offering techniques for shielding online interactions and devices.

Chapter 28: Ecology and Planetary Defense - Connects individual spiritual protection with ecological consciousness, viewing care for the Earth (Gaia) as a collective defense practice.

Chapter 29: Oaths and Pacts - Discusses the binding power of spiritual oaths and pacts, both past and present, as vibrational seals impacting protection and destiny.

Chapter 30: Integrated Self-Defense System - Advocates for combining various spiritual protection techniques into a personalized, holistic system addressing body, mind, energy field, and connection.

Prologue

At some point in the human journey, each of us senses, even without knowing how to explain it, that there is something beyond what the eyes can see. A sudden breeze that sends shivers down the spine for no reason. A weariness that cannot be justified. A sharp glance that weighs heavier than words. The invisible world doesn't just exist—it acts, reacts, and influences. And while many walk as if everything were mere matter, you stand before a book that pierces this veil and illuminates what most choose to ignore.

This is not an ordinary book. Nor is it a collection of loose beliefs or random mystical reflections. It is a true spiritual cartography. A meticulous map that traverses cultures, times, traditions, and streams of wisdom to reveal, with clarity and depth, how the invisible shapes the visible. And, even more, how you can protect, strengthen, and expand yourself from this understanding.

As you turn these pages, you won't just receive information—you will be initiated. Initiated into the art of perceiving what goes unnoticed. Of recognizing signs, cleansing your energy field, and building shields of light that cannot be found in pharmacies or gyms. This is refined ancestral wisdom, applied with mastery, that will awaken within you what has always lain dormant: the power to protect your own essence.

This work reveals what many dare not teach: that thoughts attract presences, that emotions open portals, that environments sicken not only the body but the spirit. And that, yes, there are forces that feed on your emotional weakness, your distraction, your imbalance.

It's not superstition. It's the science of the soul. And in this book, it is exposed in a living, structured, and transformative way.

You will be guided through practices that have spanned millennia: smudging that cleanses the subtle field, mantras that vibrate higher than any fear, prayers that form invisible walls, symbols that activate dormant spiritual memories. You will understand why certain sacred names hold power, why some stones are more than minerals, and why your intention—that silent force—is capable of opening or closing worlds.

But this book is not just about protection. It's about lucidity. About learning to walk through the world with awareness, discernment, presence. Because protecting oneself isn't living in fear—it's living awake. And those who awaken do not go back to sleep.

You are not here by chance. Something in you already knows there is more. You have already felt the forces no one sees. You have already noticed that certain places drain your energy, that certain thoughts are not yours, that certain people arrive like unexplained hurricanes. This book was written for those who have already intuited these truths. For those who have already sensed that the invisible also needs to be cared for, cleansed, sealed.

The reading you are about to begin is both a dive and a rescue. A dive into the deep waters of forgotten sacredness and a rescue of your own spiritual sovereignty.

Each chapter has been woven with the precision of one who knows the paths of the soul and understands that awakening is a decision. You will find legitimate knowledge here, without empty formulas, without commercial promises. Teachings born from contact with masters, rituals, traditions, and, above all, from direct experience with what is real—even if invisible.

Allow yourself to cross this threshold. Let each word cleanse, clarify, and strengthen. Let the wisdom contained herein reorganize your energy, calm your field, sharpen your perception. This book is not read only with the eyes. It is absorbed by the spirit.

It was made for those who have already felt that something needs to change. For those who no longer accept being victims of chance, envy, or the dense tides that settle without explanation. For those who want to understand how subtle forces operate and how to position themselves firmly, ethically, and with light in the face of it all.

Read attentively. Read with an open heart. Read with courage. Because after these pages, you will not be the same. The tools will be in your hands. And with them, the key to a life with more clarity, protection, and truth.

To those who feel the world is larger than taught... To those who know there is something between heaven and earth that still needs to be named... To those who wish to take command of their own spiritual field... This book is your initiation.

May you allow yourself to traverse this sacred path. With presence, with intention, with light.

Luiz Santos Editor

Chapter 1
Invisible Forces and Influences

The forces that shape human life are not limited to what the eyes see or instruments measure. Behind impulsive decisions, unexplained illnesses, and tides of misfortune that silently accumulate, pulses an invisible field, dense and ancient, where subtle forces have danced around human beings since the dawn of consciousness.

These forces, though invisible to ordinary eyes, have a real presence documented in ancient knowledge, in the traditions of peoples who lived in communion with the invisible, and in the silent accounts of those who feel—even without explanation—the weight of something that cannot be named.

In different cultures, times, and geographies, there is recognition of the existence of non-physical energies that permeate the world. The name they receive varies according to the adopted worldview: prana in Vedic India, chi in ancient China, axé in Afro-Brazilian religions, mana in Polynesian traditions. More than theoretical concepts, these energies are described as living currents, malleable, influenced by human emotions, rituals, words, and even thoughts. When these forces become misaligned or dense, an individual's life can silently collapse, without them understanding the spiritual roots of their suffering.

In the Hindu tradition, the concept of karma precisely exemplifies the logic of energetic interconnection. It is not a punitive or moralistic system, but a vibrational response to emitted actions, thoughts, and emotions. Each choice generates a reflection, and this can shape not only the present but reverberate through various incarnations. Karma can become a channel attracting harmful influences when fueled by guilt, anger, attachment, and fear. It is as if the personal frequency drops, making the spiritual field more vulnerable to invasion by destructive entities or vibrations.

In many African traditions, especially in Candomblé and Umbanda, the understanding of these forces goes beyond mere energy. There are specific entities, such as eguns and kiumbas, that take advantage of emotional and spiritual breaches to approach the living. They do not necessarily carry malice, but often remain linked to matter through traumas, unfulfilled desires, or simple ignorance of their physical death. When they find a weakened human being, emotionally or spiritually, they become energetic parasites, draining vitality and favoring disorders that doctors cannot explain.

Among indigenous peoples, these forces are respected and carefully observed. The shaman, the medicine man, acts as a mediator between worlds: physical, spiritual, dreamlike. He understands that dreams can be invasions, that sudden fever can be a warning, that the forest responds to the imbalances of the clan. For natives, the visible world is just one layer of reality. There are spirits in stones, winds, trees, and every human gesture, however simple it may seem, reverberates through the subtle fabric of existence.

In the modern West, however much life is reduced to the tangible, reports of experiences that defy logic are growing. People who feel presences in empty rooms, who fall ill without diagnosis, who face sudden drops in luck or relationships destroyed by sudden emotional chaos. Many of these phenomena are attributed to external spiritual influences—thought-forms created by other people, envy channeled like psychic arrows, spiritual obsessors who attach through emotional affinity or unconscious pacts. Some deny, some ignore, but the number of seekers looking for answers beyond matter grows with each generation.

Abrahamic religions also recognize these forces, albeit under a different vocabulary. In Christianity, there is talk of the "invisible enemy," the "spiritual hosts of wickedness," as described in Ephesians 6:12. Evil is not just a concept, but an active, intelligent presence that takes advantage of human failings to penetrate the soul and undermine its connection with the divine. Hence the importance of fasting, prayer, and faith as spiritual armor.

In Islam, the jinn are entities that inhabit a parallel dimension, created from smokeless fire, endowed with free will. Some are benign, others hostile, and many interact with humans in subtle and devastating ways.

There are specific prayers to ward them off, such as reciting Surah Al-Falaq and Al-Nas.

Spiritual interference does not only act in the field of health. There are records of dense influences causing ruptures in homes, sabotaging finances, destroying projects. This is not superstition, but the increasingly clear perception that reality is intertwined with layers of existence that respond to the emotional, ethical, and spiritual. When someone plunges into despair, they open a breach. When they lie repeatedly, they create a field of distortion. When they betray, steal, or wish ill, this field densifies with frequencies that attract beings of the same vibration. It is these beings that, invisibly, begin to influence behaviors, decisions, and destinies.

Among the ancient peoples of the Middle East, it was believed that certain places accumulated negative energy over time: cemeteries, crossroads, battlefields. These locations were avoided or "cleansed" with complex rituals. Modern science might laugh at this, but even in contemporary corporate environments, there are rooms where everyone gets sick, spaces that generate discouragement, places where productivity dies. The vibrational field of the environment, fed by past emotions and events, remains impregnated, acting as a silent agent in the degradation of the physical and mental health of those who stay there for long periods.

Astrology, in turn, shows how celestial bodies—whose gravity and magnetism are invisible to the naked eye—influence births, cycles, behaviors. Mars in conflict with Saturn can indicate a period of friction and tension, not only psychological but spiritual. An eclipse can open portals, and certain planetary conjunctions are seen as moments of energetic risk. It is not about a fixed destiny, but predispositions that, if not observed, can amplify hidden vulnerabilities.

Spiritual life is not neutral. The absence of protective practices, self-knowledge, ethical and vibrational alignment creates a state of exposure. The human being, like a poorly tuned radio, begins to pick up noise from beyond. These noises manifest as destructive thoughts that do not belong to the original mind, attitudes that sabotage one's own evolution, addictions that are not only physical but spiritual. Many live entire lives under the influence of these forces, believing they are their choices, when in fact they are puppets of an invisible programming that operates through energetic affinity.

Just as stagnant water attracts mosquitoes, a spiritual field without movement, without light, without prayer or awareness, attracts entities that survive on the energy of others. These are the so-called astral larvae, miasmas, obsessors—each tradition with its name, but all pointing to the same phenomenon: forms of life or thought that attach to humans through points of weakness, unhealed traumas, unacknowledged pains.

Understanding these forces is the first step. Recognizing that the world is much more than the visible is not a sign of weakness or superstition, but of ancestral wisdom lost in excessive rationalism. Relearning to feel the invisible, to cleanse the field, to seal the energy body, and to keep the inner light burning—all this will be necessary for spiritual protection to become a living part of daily life.

There is no neutral space in this world. Where there is no conscious light, darkness settles. Where there is no voice of the soul, the noise of the external governs. From the moment one recognizes the existence and influence of invisible forces, a profound review of how one lives, feels, and interacts with the world becomes inevitable. The responsibility for one's own energy field becomes non-transferable, demanding an active stance from the individual regarding spiritual life. It is not just about defending against the negative, but cultivating what elevates: lucidity, presence, clear intention. This implies constant practices of energetic self-care, from observing one's own thoughts to refining companionships, spoken words, frequented environments. Every daily gesture, however banal it may seem, carries the power to tune frequencies.

Understanding these forces also requires humility. No matter how much one studies or experiments, the invisible world does not bend to linear logic nor fit into simplified mental models. Intuition, subtle listening, signs that arrive in dreams or synchronicities—all this gains value and weight. To live under this awareness is to accept that we are in constant relation with what is unseen, and that there are intelligences, memories, and presences that cross time and space to interact with us. Cultivating spirituality, therefore, is strengthening this relationship—not as a paranoid shield, but as a sacred bond with the deeper reality of existence.

Spiritual vigilance, when combined with self-knowledge, transforms into freedom. And this freedom is not the absence of influences, but the ability to discern them, welcome them, or push them away with wisdom. The human being who understands their role in the great invisible fabric of life learns to walk more lightly, even amidst darkness. They do not deny the shadows, but light candles. And thus, remain whole.

Chapter 2
The Power of Intention

Intention is a silent seed dwelling at the core of human actions, and its power echoes beyond time, beyond flesh. Long before any word is spoken, even before a gesture materializes, intention already pulses in the invisible field, shaping the course of events and attracting forces compatible with its original vibration. Within the spiritual arts of protection, intention is not just one tool among many: it is the very foundation upon which any shield, ritual, or enchantment is built.

No amulet, mantra, or symbol holds intrinsic power if not activated by a living, clear, and firm intention. This truth, repeated in diverse mystical traditions, spans the ages like a golden thread connecting the magicians of ancient Egypt to the monks of Tibet, indigenous healers to masters of modern occultism. Directed will is the spark that awakens dormant forces in the fabric of the universe. It is from intention that portals open or close, that paths are illuminated or obscured.

In Tibetan Buddhism, the practice of visualization is a refinement of this applied intention. Monks are trained from an early age to project mental images of protective deities, purifying lights, or sacred mandalas.

This is not passive imagination, but an energetic construction that comes alive in the mind and expands into the surrounding space. The clarity of the mental image, the discipline of breathing, and the firmness of intention create a protective field around the practitioner—a field that repels hostile entities, obsessive thoughts, and dissonant vibrations.

Similarly, in forest shamanism, intention is the key to every spiritual journey. The shaman, preparing a smudge, relies not only on the smoke of the herb. He breathes his intention, his request, his life force into it. Upon entering an altered state of consciousness, whether through drumming, ayahuasca, or deep silence, he carries the intention of healing, seeking, or liberation. Without this inner direction, spirits may manifest, but the ritual does not fulfill its purpose. The forest responds to the heart's intention, not the empty words of the mouth.

In contemporary Neopaganism, especially in the Wiccan tradition, intention is formally taught as the central element of every spell. Modern witches see magic not as a theatrical act, but as a vibrational pact between humans and the forces of nature. A protection spell may involve candles, herbs, and crystals, but what activates it is the conscious direction of will. When a witch casts a magic circle, she is not just defining a physical space: she is sealing an intention that shapes space-time and wards off any unwanted interference.

Affirmations, in turn, are a verbalized form of intention. Repeated with presence and belief, they not only reinforce positive beliefs but transform the personal energy field. An affirmation like "I am protected by the divine light that surrounds me" creates a vibrational layer around the body, like an invisible force field. When repeated daily, with focus and emotion, this affirmation acts as a spiritual password, a reminder to the unconscious and the universe that this being is not vulnerable, but conscious and protected.

Modern science, though skeptical of spiritual languages, is beginning to decipher the effects of intention on matter. Experiments with water crystals, like those conducted by Masaru Emoto, demonstrate how words and thoughts affect the molecular structure of water. If human intention can alter a molecule, it can also influence the vibrations of the subtle field. Neuroscience studies also show how mentalization can alter brain patterns, immunity, and emotional states. Even without calling it magic, science recognizes: the focused mind modifies the body and the environment.

Exercising intention is, therefore, training in presence. It is the opposite of the mental dispersion that dominates modern daily life. To activate protective intention, one must withdraw from the noise, anchor in the present moment, and clearly declare what is desired. It is not enough to want. One must want with the totality of being. Divided intention is a half-open door to interference. Firm intention is a wall of light that does not break.

A powerful ancestral practice consists of visualizing golden light. Closing the eyes, breathing deeply three times, and visualizing a sphere of golden light originating in the center of the chest. With the force of intention, this light expands, fills the entire body, and then forms a cocoon around the being. Within this sphere, no negative force penetrates. This practice, when performed daily, strengthens the energy field and attunes the individual to higher frequencies. The sphere of light is both symbolic and real on the subtle plane. Its effectiveness depends less on the perfection of the mental image and more on the intensity of the intention.

Another exercise is that of the blue flame of protection. Used in Western esoteric schools, such as the White Brotherhood, this technique invokes the energy of Archangel Michael. The practice consists of visualizing a cobalt-blue flame enveloping the body, burning away all negativity and sealing the auric field. Repeating the name "Michael" sequentially, in a low voice or mentally, acts as a vibrational anchor. The name becomes a mantra. And the mantra is, par excellence, the verbalization of sacred intention.

It is important to understand that intention is not limited to protection against external evil. It also acts as an internal filter. When one truly desires to live with ethics, integrity, and light, the very vibration of the being changes. And like attracts like. The higher the intention governing someone's life, the lower the possibility of attracting dense entities. Not because they don't exist, but because there is no resonance. The field of elevated intention is like music that low-vibration spirits cannot bear to hear.

Ceremonial magic traditions teach that before any ritual, the practitioner must define their "greater purpose." This purpose is the anchor of the magical operation. If it is confused, selfish, or unstable, the ritual will fail or attract unpredictable consequences. The universe responds precisely to the emitted intention. Therefore, when asking for protection, it is necessary to do so clearly. Protection from what? For what purpose? With what motivation? This is not paranoia, but spiritual lucidity. Intention does not lie, and the invisible plane responds to its essence.

In the Sufi tradition of Islam, intention (niyyah) is considered the heart of all spiritual action. Even if a ritual is perfectly executed, without the correct niyyah, it is empty. The Sufi is taught to purify intention before each prayer, each act, each step. He seeks protection not only for himself but to be more aligned with the divine will. This purity of intention is seen as a shield against any spiritual attack, for a transparent heart offers no mirrors where evil can reflect itself.

In the silence of the early morning, when the world sleeps and the soul awakens, intention becomes almost palpable. It is in this liminal state between sleep and wakefulness that mentalization exercises gain extraordinary strength. The mind is malleable, and the spiritual field more receptive. The practice of visualizing protection upon waking and before sleeping creates an energetic routine that teaches the spiritual body to remain attentive. It is like training an invisible muscle, which gradually becomes firm and instinctive.

Recognizing intention as a primary force makes it evident that reality is not a stage for mechanical performance, but a mirror responding to inner vibration. This vibration, fueled by clarity of purpose and commitment to inner truth, radiates like an invisible code, encoding the experiences around it. When intention is guided by the ego, paths become tortuous; but when shaped by a deep listening of the soul, it transforms into a compass. At this point, the human being ceases to react to circumstances and begins to co-create, no longer a hostage to chance, but conscious of their own energetic emission into the fabric of life.

The power of intention also reveals that any spiritual practice, however simple, can achieve unsuspected potential when nurtured with meaning. A glass of water can become a healing elixir, a lit candle can illuminate inner paths, a whispered prayer can ward off invisible storms—everything depends on the vibrational quality of the intention behind the act. It is not about accumulating esoteric gestures, but about making every gesture a rite, every word a seal, every thought a clear direction. And thus, daily life becomes spiritualized, not by denying matter, but by the intentional gaze that consecrates the ordinary with purpose.

True spiritual protection, therefore, arises from the coherence between what is desired, what is thought, and what is lived. When intention and action walk in unison, the energy field aligns with greater forces, and a subtle serenity begins to guide decisions. It is not armor against the world, but a state of attunement that transforms the being itself into living light. From there, protection ceases to be an external effort and becomes a constant presence—silent, firm, and inevitable.

Chapter 3
Sacred Symbols

There is a language that belongs to no nation, yet is understood by all sensitive souls: symbols. They are not mere drawings, nor decorations from an ancient time. They are living structures holding layers of spiritual and vibrational knowledge. Each line, each curve, each geometric shape carries an energetic history, its own frequency, and a specific function. In the context of spiritual protection, symbols are portals and shields, they are watchful eyes, cutting swords, repelling bucklers. It is no coincidence that where true faith exists, there is also a symbol engraved, carved, drawn, or worn close to the body.

The cross, for example, is far from being just a Christian emblem. Long before being associated with the sacrifice of Christ, it appeared in ancient civilizations representing the intersection point between heaven and earth, spirit and matter. In Egypt, there was the ankh, or crux ansata, a symbol of eternal life and divine life force. Early Christians, by adopting the cross, were consciously or unconsciously anchoring themselves in a millennial archetype of divine intercession. When used with intention and reverence, the cross is not just a symbol of faith: it becomes a seal of protection against forces contrary to light. Whether on the neck, on the wall, or traced in the air, it anchors the presence of the sacred.

The Eye of Horus, in turn, spans millennia as one of the most powerful known symbols of protection. Originating in ancient Egypt, it is the all-seeing eye, perceiving the invisible and revealing the hidden. Egyptian priests used it not only as an ornament but as a seal against hostile forces, such as astral entities and curses cast by black magic. Its symmetry is not just aesthetic—it mirrors the balance between hemispheres, the harmony between reason and intuition. When activated with awareness, the Eye of Horus acts as a spiritual sentinel, keeping away influences that attempt to operate in the shadows.

Another widely used symbol is the Hand of Fatima, also known as Hamsa. Present in Islam, Judaism, and even North African traditions, this open hand points to the power of divine intercession, justice, and protection against the evil eye. In the Islamic context, it is linked to the Prophet Muhammad's daughter, Fatima Zahra, carrying deep symbolism of faith, honor, and firmness. In Judaism, it is called the Hand of Miriam, Moses' sister, and associated with the protective force of the number five. Whether with an eye in the center, inscriptions of sacred verses, or just its simple outline, the Hamsa is one of the oldest and most effective talismans against envy, intrigue, and spiritual attacks.

Mandalas, meanwhile, emerge as geometric expressions of the cosmos. In Hindu and Buddhist traditions, they are not just drawings—they are sacred maps, spiritual architectures that, when contemplated or drawn, align the energy field and block negative interference. Each color, each symmetry, each central point has an anchoring function. When placed in environments, they act as centers of balance and purification. Meditating before a mandala with the intention of protection activates a vibrational network that strengthens the practitioner's subtle shield.

Within African traditions, especially Voodoo and Candomblé, symbols take shape in *pontos riscados* (chalk drawings) and the symbols of the orishas. Exu, Ogum, Oxóssi, Yemanjá—each entity has its spiritual signature, its unique trace that summons and anchors it. By drawing these points with *pemba* powder or other sacred powders, a barrier is created, a line of force separating the consecrated space from the rest of the world. What is drawn with respect and knowledge cannot be trespassed with impunity. It is as if the symbols themselves gain life and become spiritual soldiers on constant watch.

In Kabbalah, the use of Hebrew letters, especially divine names, functions as a defense mechanism against external influences. Yod-He-Vav-He, the sacred tetragrammaton, is more than a name: it is a combination of frequencies that, when written or pronounced with reverence, alters the vibration of space and being. Kabbalistic symbols engraved on parchments, metals, or stones have been used for centuries to seal homes, protect objects, and shield people against wandering spirits and dense energies.

But a symbol, to be effective, must be activated. It is not enough to wear an Eye of Horus around the neck or hang a mandala on the wall. Activation is the process of connection between the symbol, the user's intention, and the higher forces it represents. It can be done through prayer, consecration with water, smudging with herbs, or even simple meditation where one visualizes the symbol emanating light and spinning at a high frequency. Activation is the moment the symbol awakens. Until then, it is inert matter. Afterward, it becomes a channel.

Each symbol has its language. Some must be placed facing a specific direction. Others should never be exposed to the gaze of the curious. There are those worn close to the body and those that must be buried or burned after use. Ignorance of these practices can neutralize or even reverse the desired effect. Therefore, when working with protective symbols, respect and study are crucial. Trivializing the sacred opens doors. Conscious use seals portals.

Some symbols are considered dangerous when handled by unprepared hands. The pentagram, for example, is commonly associated with black magic, but it is actually one of the oldest symbols of protection and spiritual balance. It represents the five elements: earth, fire, water, air, and spirit. When pointing upwards, it indicates the supremacy of spirit over matter, creating a field of order and harmony. Inverted, however, it distorts towards uncontrolled materiality, becoming a channel for unbalanced forces. The symbol itself is neither good nor bad. It is a mirror of the intention that animates it.

Celtic shields, engraved with endless knots and zoomorphic figures, are also vibrational tools. Each knot, each interweaving, represents the continuous flow of life, the interconnection between worlds, and protection through ancestral wisdom. In ancient times, these designs were tattooed on warriors' bodies, engraved on battle shields, and carved into temple doors. Not as art, but as visual enchantments. They still retain this function today, provided they are treated for what they are: keys to ancient knowledge.

In some lines of contemporary magic, especially chaos magic, personalized sigils are created from power phrases. A person formulates an affirmation—for example, "Nothing can harm me"—eliminates repeated letters, and rearranges the strokes until a new symbol is created. This sigil is then charged with emotional energy, whether through meditation, visualization, or ritual acts. The result is a unique symbol, created for a specific purpose, with high power for protection and energetic alignment.

The relationship with symbols should be intimate. They are not collector's items, nor esoteric fads. They are mirrors of the spirit, windows to greater realities. When choosing a symbol for protection, it is important to observe which one resonates with the soul. There is no symbol better than another—there is the one that speaks most strongly to your essence. It is this attunement that enhances the connection, making the symbol living and operative.

The presence of symbols in daily spiritual life serves not only to ward off dangers but also to constantly remind us of who we are and what we seek to preserve. They operate as visible anchors of an invisible reality, helping maintain the soul's focus when the external world tries to distract and disperse. Having a symbol nearby is often an act of fidelity to an inner pact—with light, with truth, with one's own evolution. The symbol is a silent witness to the intention that invokes it, and therefore demands responsibility. Its power lies not only in the ancestral trace but in the energy of the one who activates it and the coherence of its use.

Throughout history, entire civilizations have risen based on symbols. They were engraved on stones, fabrics, bodies, and weapons not merely as ornaments or signs of belonging, but as forms of alignment with greater forces. Today, despite the excess of information and the superficiality with which sacred elements are treated, it is still possible to cultivate a deep relationship with these primordial forms. This requires time, listening, practice, and respect. A symbol, once understood in its essence, becomes part of the vibrational field of the one who carries it. It is no longer an adornment—it is an extension of the soul, a garment of light overlaying the physical body. It is in this communion between symbol and spirit that true protection is born. When one looks at a sacred trace and recognizes in it not just a drawing, but a mirror of one's own journey, then the symbol fulfills its role. It silences noise, wards off chaos, and keeps the presence of the sacred alive and pulsating. The soul protected by conscious symbols is not shielded against challenges, but strengthened to face them with courage, lucidity, and faith. And that is enough.

Chapter 4
Prayer and Christian Faith

There are words that do not get lost in the wind. They rise like invisible incense, traverse the layers of the world, and touch what lies beyond time. Prayer, when born from a sincere heart, is both a sword and a shield, a breath of light capable of piercing the densest darkness. At the heart of the Christian tradition, it is not mere supplication: it is presence, a living connection with the Holy Spirit, a fortress erected between man and the assaults of evil. Faith, in turn, is the soil where this prayer flourishes. Without faith, words are hollow sounds. With faith, they become walls that no opposing force can breach.

From the earliest centuries of Christianity, prayer was understood as a practice of protection. The desert monks, facing temptations and dark visions, did not wield weapons, but psalms. The Word was their armor. And among all sacred texts, Psalm 91 became the quintessential bastion for those facing the invisible. "He who dwells in the secret place of the Most High shall abide under the shadow of the Almighty"—there is no verse more known among those who take refuge in divine strength. Its power lies not just in the sound, but in the spiritual authority it carries. Repeated with faith, it seals the spirit, dispels presences, strengthens morale.

The Catholic tradition preserves ancient mechanisms of spiritual protection that go beyond spontaneous prayer. Holy water, for example, is considered a sacramental—not because it contains inherent virtue, but because it is linked to the Church's blessing and the faith of the one using it. When sprinkled in environments or on the body, it not only purifies but creates a vibrational field that repels hostile entities. Exorcists commonly use it as a tool for banishment. There are reports of violent manifestations by obsessors merely at the touch of consecrated water, clear evidence that what seems like mere liquid actually carries the memory of the divine covenant.

The cross, traced in the air or on the body, is another widely recognized protective gesture. By making the sign of the cross, the faithful invoke the Trinity: Father, Son, and Holy Spirit. But beyond the invocation, a sacred mark is traced on the spiritual field. When made consciously, the cross becomes a key for energetic closure, a seal against invisible assaults. Many old priests recommended that, upon sensing strange presences, the faithful trace the cross upon themselves and chant the name of Jesus, for there is no name above His. The forces acting in shadow tremble before the light invoked by the Name.

The New Testament also offers a spiritual arsenal. In Ephesians 6:11-18, Paul speaks of the "armor of God," calling believers to dress spiritually to resist the "wiles of the devil." He describes the belt of truth, the breastplate of righteousness, the shield of faith, the helmet of salvation, the sword of the Spirit—which is the Word—and feet shod with the readiness of the gospel. Each element of this armor is symbolic, but its ritualistic use is real. Many faithful, before sleeping or upon waking, visualize each part of the armor being put on. This is not vain imagination, but vibrational construction that protects the auric field against harmful influences.

Among Protestants, prayer is often more spontaneous, but no less powerful for it. Pentecostals, in particular, speak of "fervent prayer," the kind that comes from the depths of the spirit, often accompanied by tears, trembling, and glories. It is the prayer that breaks chains, touches heaven, and dispels any shadowy presence. Many ministries teach prayer in tongues as a form of shielding—an unknown language the soul uses to communicate directly with God, without interference from intercepting entities.

Another powerful element is praise. Singing hymns, chanting psalms, listening to sacred music—all elevate the vibration of the environment, driving away miasmas and obsessors. There are homes whose energy field changes completely just by constantly playing worship music. The atmosphere purifies, thoughts become lighter, emotions organize. Sincere praise is not just sound—it is divine frequency.

We must also not forget the Lord's Prayer. Taught by Christ himself, it contains profound spiritual keys. By saying "deliver us from evil," the one praying is not just asking for protection against visible dangers, but sealing their field against invisible evil. When said with full awareness, this prayer forms a circle of light around the being, connecting them with the divine and excluding all unwanted influence.

Some more advanced practitioners also use the rosary as an instrument of protection. Each Hail Mary, each Our Father, each Glory Be is a stone placed in the wall of faith. Repetitive prayers are not vain—they are sacred drums that set the rhythm of the spiritual field. The rosary, when prayed with devotion, creates such a high vibration that hostile entities withdraw. It is a common practice among exorcists and intercessors.

Christian faith teaches that no opposing force prevails against a surrendered heart. Spiritual protection, on this path, is not made only of rituals or words, but of a consecrated life. A being who walks in righteousness, who forgives, who loves, who serves, who prays truthfully, is forbidden territory to darkness. Because where the Spirit of God dwells, there is no room for shadow.

Prayer, when cultivated as a habit and not just an emergency resource, transforms into a permanent atmosphere. It shapes the home, the body, relationships, and even silences. It is not an automatic repetition, but an inner posture that extends beyond words. A home where prayer is frequent is a home where the invisible finds natural barriers against evil, like walls built with bricks of light. Similarly, a mind trained by constant prayer becomes less vulnerable to subtle attacks of negativity, as its frequency rises even before danger approaches.

Christian prayer, throughout the centuries, has proven effective not only through its rituals but through the strength of the presence it invokes. Jesus, teaching the Lord's Prayer, did not offer a closed code, but a model of alignment with divine will. Every prayer made with surrender is a return to the source, an opening of the field for grace to flow. When the name of Christ is called with faith, it becomes both shield and sword. That is why, even in the most extreme episodes—serious illnesses, emotional crises, spiritual oppressions—Christian faith has sustained millions. Not by magic, but because light always responds when evoked truthfully.

On this path, the greatest protection lies not only in the words spoken or practices performed but in the inner state of the one praying. A life aligned with the love of Christ, compassion, forgiveness, and truth becomes itself a living prayer, exuding light wherever it goes. Prayer and faith do not end with the devotional moment but extend to gesture, thought, daily choice. And when this happens, evil finds no breaches, for everything there already belongs to the light. And where light reigns, evil dissipates.

Chapter 5
Amulets in Islam

In the heart of the ancient desert sands, where light and darkness have waged silent disputes since the dawn of revelation, lie the secrets of Islamic protection. There, amidst the echoes of the Quran and the winds whispering God's name in every grain, Muslims learned that the invisible is real and its influence is fought not with brute force, but with upright faith and pure invocation. In Islam, spiritual protection is not an accessory; it is the very foundation of existence. From birth to the last breath, the believer is taught to take refuge in Allah against all that cannot be seen.

The Quran, the sacred book of Islam, is considered by the faithful not just scripture, but a living presence, a source of light, and a shield against all forms of hidden evil. Each verse, in itself, is a vibrational field emitting protection to those who recite it with sincerity and reverence. Among all protective passages, one stands out as a bastion: Ayat al-Kursi, or the Verse of the Throne, which constitutes verse 255 of Surah Al-Baqarah. Recited with faith, this verse invokes the absolute sovereignty of Allah, His power to watch over everything without ever tiring, and His light that cannot be suppressed. Many Muslims recite Ayat al-Kursi after obligatory prayers, upon leaving home, before sleeping, and in moments of spiritual unease. The power contained in this passage is so recognized that, in various Islamic cultures, it is written on paper, cloth, metal, and even temporary tattoos, carried close to the body or affixed to walls and doors. The verse, when chanted with pure intention, is like a sword of light tearing through the veil of negative influences, dissolving enchantments, envy, obsessions, and jinn—spiritual entities described in the Quran as invisible and possessing free will.

The jinn, recurring figures in Islamic cosmology, are creatures made of smokeless fire. They share the world with humans but inhabit a parallel dimension. They can be Muslim or not, peaceful or hostile. Those who stray from divine light are often accused of causing mental confusion, mysterious illnesses, persistent nightmares, and even possessions. Islam naturally acknowledges their existence and offers clear methods for dealing with these entities: prayer, fasting, recitation of the Quran, and invocation of God's name—"Bismillah" (In the name of Allah) being the first shield pronounced before any important action.

Surahs Al-Falaq and An-Nas, known as the surahs of refuge, are another powerful resource for protection. They comprise the last two chapters of the Quran and were revealed, according to tradition, specifically to heal Prophet Muhammad from a spell cast against him. Reciting them sequentially, especially at dawn, dusk, and before sleep, is like building an invisible fortress around the soul. Al-Falaq calls for protection against what was created with malice, against the darkness that subtly infiltrates, against sorcery, and against the envious eye. An-Nas, in turn, seeks refuge in the Lord of humanity against the whispering evil forces inhabiting the invisible.

Beyond recitations, many Muslims adopt the use of physical amulets, although this custom is shrouded in controversy. In Sunni Islam, particularly in Salafist and Wahhabi currents, the use of talismans is strongly discouraged, considered shirk—a form of associating something with God, which is the greatest sin in Islamic monotheism. For these groups, any protection not coming exclusively from direct faith in Allah is a dangerous deviation.

However, among popular Muslims, especially in regions of North Africa, the Indian subcontinent, and the Middle East, the tradition of amulets persists, blending pre-Islamic and mystical practices with orthodox Islam. Such amulets, known as "ta'wiz," are small capsules or folded cloths containing verses from the Quran, divine names, or specific invocations written by a scholar or spiritual leader. They are sewn into fabrics, attached with cords, or inserted into metal pendants, usually worn around the neck, arm, or waist. Their power, devotees believe, comes from the purity of the writer and the faith of the wearer. It is not fetishism, but a constant reminder of the divine presence—a way to keep the mind and heart focused on the protection that comes from above.

There is also the Hand of Fatima, or Khamsa, whose use has spread through Islamic and Jewish cultures. Although its origin predates Islam, it was incorporated as a symbol of protection against the evil eye, attributed to Fatima Zahra, the Prophet's daughter. The outstretched hand, often drawn with an eye in the center, represents strength, patience, and faith. Despite its mystical and possibly pre-Islamic roots, it is commonly seen in homes, clothing, and jewelry, especially among Muslim women, as a visual barrier against envy and negativity.

Another recurring resource is the use of the name "Allah" in Arabic calligraphy, displayed in homes, cars, places of business. The constant visualization of this holy name is, in itself, a reminder that no force has real power except the Creator. The presence of this name in the environment is seen as a lamp against spiritual darkness. There is no superstition in this gesture, but a recognition of the importance of dhikr—the constant remembrance of God, which acts as continuous protection against distractions and invisible attacks.

Within Shiism, especially among Sufis, there is a more open relationship with amulets and talismans. Sufis see the universe as a reflection of the divine and believe certain objects can contain barakah—a kind of accumulated spiritual blessing, whether through contact with a saint, use in prayer, or carrying sacred symbols. Stones like red agate (aqeeq), often engraved with the names of imams or Quranic verses, are worn by many Shiites as protective rings. It is believed they repel evil and strengthen the faith of the wearer.

Sufis also use mystical prayers, called "awrad," recited daily as spiritual protection. Many of these formulas come from ancient lineages, passed down from master to disciple, carrying vibrational codes of immense power. When chanted in a light trance state, with the heart in purity and the body in stillness, these words become sonic shields strengthening the devotee's energy field.

Although Islam warns against blind dependence on physical objects, it never underestimates the power of intention and the sacred word. Thus, true protection resides not in the talisman itself, but in the trusting heart. What protects is not the metal, the cloth, the stone, but the living remembrance that Allah is Al-Hafiz—the Protector, the Guardian, the one who watches even when human eyes sleep.

The essence of protection in Islam, therefore, lies not in external elements, but in the constant awareness of divine presence. The ta'wiz, the agate ring, the name of Allah engraved on walls—all these are tangible reflections of an inner relationship with the sacred. When understood as extensions of dhikr, prayer, and right intention, these objects become more than adornments: they become bridges between the visible and the invisible, silent reminders that no darkness can resist the light of one truly anchored in God. And it is this awareness, more than any form, that separates the devout from the superstitious.

Even amidst theological disagreements about the use of amulets, there is a shared certainty among all branches of Islam: it is the constant remembrance of Allah that seals the heart against evil. Sufis, with their ecstatic chants and deep devotional practices, Salafists with their emphasis on doctrinal purity and direct recitation of the Quran—all recognize, in their own way, that spiritual evil only finds breaches where there is forgetfulness, negligence, dispersion. The true shield is active faith, the vigilant heart, the tongue that never tires of saying "Bismillah" before each step. For every gesture begun in the name of God carries within it a shield that traverses worlds.

Thus, amidst sacred stones and Quranic verses, between the Hand of Fatima and faith-filled silence, the Muslim walks not as one avoiding evil out of fear, but as one trusting in the Protector's shelter. Protection in Islam is surrender, not control. It is a serene vigilance that acknowledges invisible dangers but refuses to fear them, knowing that above all evil there is a Name that sees all, knows all, and guards all. And it is in this Name that the heart rests securely.

Chapter 6
Hindu Mantras and Yantras

There is a point in space where sound touches light and form bends before vibration. It is in this subtle place, where common senses fail, that the mantras and yantras of Hinduism are born. More than sacred formulas or images, they are energetic codes that shape reality, seal the spiritual field, and create protective structures that cannot be breached by human hands or presences from the invisible world. They are ancient spiritual technologies, inherited from the Vedas, perpetuated not just as part of a religion, but as a path of alignment with the primordial force of the universe.

At the heart of the Vedic tradition, vibration is considered the fundamental substance of the cosmos. "Nada Brahma"—sound is God. The universe was created by a primordial sound, and since then, everything vibrates, everything resonates, everything responds to the hidden rhythm of being. Mantras are pure expressions of this truth. Each syllable, each phoneme, was discovered by rishis in altered states of consciousness and rigorously preserved for thousands of years, as they alter not only the practitioner's mind but the energetic fabric of the environment where they are chanted.

Among all mantras, the most universal and well-known is Om (Aum). It represents the primordial vibration, the sound of the birth, maintenance, and dissolution of the universe. Chanted with full presence, Om is not just a sound, but a wave that resonates on three planes: physical, mental, and spiritual. By vibrating Om, the body aligns, the mind silences, and the subtle field expands. It is common in ashrams and temples for the recitation of Om to precede any other ritual, as it cleanses the space and wards off any invisible interferences.

Another mantra of immeasurable protective power is the Gayatri. Considered the mother of all mantras, it invokes Savitur, the cosmic sun, source of all intelligence and life. Its regular recitation is prescribed in the Vedas as an essential practice for those seeking protection, wisdom, and enlightenment. These are words that call upon the higher light to penetrate the reciter's mind, purifying them of negative influences, dispelling shadows, and establishing a vibrational fortress around them. In its best-known form, the Gayatri is recited thus:

"Om Bhur Bhuvah Swaha Tat Savitur Varenyam Bhargo Devasya Dheemahi Dhiyo Yonah Prachodayat."

Each verse of this mantra is like a ray of light cutting through the veils of ignorance, and when chanted with devotion, it transforms the body into a temple, the voice into a sword, and the heart into a shield.

Besides mantras, the Hindu tradition offers yantras—geometric diagrams that, at first glance, seem like intricate patterns. But each line, each angle, each central point has a specific purpose. Yantras are spiritual architectures drawn in two dimensions that mirror protective structures from more subtle planes. They are, in essence, abodes of the gods. When activated with mantra, intention, and concentration, they become highly powerful energy fields, capable of repelling any adverse entity or influence.

The most well-known of all yantras is the Sri Yantra. Formed by nine interconnected triangles radiating from a central point, it represents the cosmos and the human body in relation to the divine. Its center, the bindu, is the gateway to the absolute. By meditating on the Sri Yantra, the practitioner immerses themselves in a field of energy so dense and ordered that their own energetic structure reorganizes. Many yogis use it not only for protection but for dissolving karmas, warding off obsessors, and integrating with cosmic consciousness.

There are also yantras dedicated to specific deities, such as the yantra of Kali, the dark goddess of the destruction of the ego and demonic forces. When activated, this yantra summons Kali's energy as a guardian. It is not uncommon for devotees to use it in times of intense spiritual warfare, when they feel surrounded by hostile presences or in environments permeated by dense energies. Kali does not hesitate— her presence is overwhelming, destructive of all falsehood. Her yantra is, therefore, a seal of fire that burns everything attempting to infiltrate.

The activation of mantras and yantras does not occur through mechanical repetition or casual drawing. It requires preparation, purity of intention, vibrational alignment, and ideally, transmission by a master. Many gurus teach that the mantra should be received directly, as it carries the shakti—the living energy of the spiritual lineage. When transmitted consciously, the mantra becomes an extension of the master within the disciple, protecting them as if the master themselves were present in their aura.

In tantric practices, the use of mantras and yantras is even deeper. Each chakra of the body is activated with specific sounds—bija mantras—which, when chanted correctly, seal the energy centers against invasions. Lam, Vam, Ram, Yam, Ham, Om, are the seed sounds corresponding to the seven main centers. These sounds awaken the kundalini, the serpentine force dormant at the base of the spine, and when this force rises unblocked, no negative entity remains in the practitioner's field. The light becomes total.

Offerings to deities are also part of the protective tradition. The invocation of Hanuman, the monkey god, is a classic example. A symbol of strength, fidelity, and courage, Hanuman is called upon in moments of fear, possession, or spiritual warfare. His mantra, "Om Hanumate Namah," is repeated by thousands of devotees seeking protection. It is said that where Hanuman is remembered with devotion, the very air purifies, and negative forces flee like shadows before the rising sun.

For those seeking protection in times of chaos and internal disorder, the mantra of Narasimha, the leonine form of Vishnu, is a spiritual remedy. The mantra "Om Namo Bhagavate Narasimhaya" invokes the destroyer of demons, the defender of devotees, the one who appears with flaming claws when injustice crosses the line. Many priests recommend chanting this mantra in homes where there are baseless screams, frequent nightmares, or a sense of strange presence. Narasimha, once invoked, never retreats.

In traditional rituals, mantras are chanted around sacred fires, while yantras are drawn with colored powder or engraved on copper plates. But even in the silence of a simple room, the power of these tools remains. What matters is the purity of intention, the focus of the mind, the true desire for light. The Hindu tradition judges not the pomp, but the surrender. The deity responds not to external grandeur, but to internal vibration.

In modern times, it is common to see people chanting mantras in guided meditations, tattooing yantras on their bodies, or decorating their homes with these sacred geometries. But caution is needed. A mantra pronounced disrespectfully, a yantra displayed without activation, are like dull swords or open gates. Form without spirit is just form. It must be remembered that these practices are alive, and only respond to the living presence of those who invoke them.

Understanding the living nature of mantras and yantras makes it clear that their use goes beyond spiritual aesthetics or mere repetition. They are direct pathways to divine archetypes, subtle intelligences, and cosmic patterns that structure reality. Their strength lies not in the isolated form or sound, but in the synergy between sound, intention, and consciousness. A mantra chanted with an absent heart does not reach the higher planes, just as a yantra drawn irreverently does not pulse with energy. The effectiveness of these practices is rooted in presence—the same presence that permeated the rishis discovering sacred sounds and sustains the invisible link between the seeker and the divine.

In this sense, true spiritual protection is not just a shield against evil, but an internal reorganization that aligns us with cosmic order. When the body vibrates to the sound of the mantra and the mind focuses on the geometry of the yantra, inner chaos dissipates and clarity settles. Fear, doubt, and the feeling of separation dissolve in the frequency of unity. In a world where so many voices compete for attention and subtle forces operate invisibly, returning to these ancestral pillars is also an act of luminous resistance, a way to rekindle the sacred fire burning silently within every awakened being.

Thus, the path of mantras and yantras demands not only knowledge but humility and surrender. They are tools that respond to inner truth, flourishing when watered with sincere devotion. Each syllable chanted consciously, each line drawn intentionally, is a step towards the center—that point where sound touches light and the invisible bows before the awakened presence. In that place, protection is no longer a necessity, but a natural consequence of the state of communion.

Chapter 7
Ancestral Smudging

There exists an invisible link between aroma and spirit. The moment smoke rises, in spirals that seem to dance into another dimension, the world transforms. The air purifies, time alters, and the invisible reveals itself. Smudging is not just an ancient custom—it is an ancestral language, an olfactory code communicating to spirituality that something is being sealed, cleansed, consecrated. It is fire that transforms, smoke that transits between worlds, herb that sings. At its core, smudging is a silent pact between the human and the divine, where the plant element lends its soul so the spirit may find order and protection.

Long before candles were lit or magic circles drawn, herbs were already being burned. In the caves of the first tribes, in the tents of shamans, in Afro-Brazilian *terreiros*, in the hidden altars of alchemists, and in the wrinkled hands of healers, fire and smoke were the first sacred words. Smudging, therefore, is universal. Where there is true spirituality, there is rising smoke. It not only wards off what is impure but opens paths, calls allies, seals portals, establishes vibrational order where chaos once reigned.

Among the indigenous peoples of the Americas, smudging is a ritual for purifying the body, soul, home, and territory. White sage is one of the most sacred herbs for the native nations of North America. When burned, it is considered a messenger between worlds. The smoke carries prayers to the Great Spirit and dispels entities hiding in the invisible crevices of space. Before sacred ceremonies, participants are smudged from head to toe, including sacred objects, healing instruments, and even animals present. Nothing enters a circle of power without first passing through the sieve of smoke.

In the traditions of Candomblé and Umbanda, smudging plays a central role in preparing the ritual space. No *gira*, no work, no spiritual consultation begins before the environment is properly smudged. The chosen herbs vary according to the session's purpose: rue, guinea-hen weed, rosemary, lavender, benzoin, myrrh, frankincense. Each of these plants possesses a specific vibration, an energetic signature that, when burned, activates certain frequencies. Their combination is made with ancestral knowledge. When mixed, the herbs compose true spells of purification, expulsion, or attraction of spiritual forces.

Rue, for example, is considered one of the strongest herbs for warding off negative energies. Its scent is penetrating, and its vibration acts directly on spiritual channels that accumulate densities. By burning rue, the practitioner not only cleanses the environment but also cuts invisible ties, dissolves miasmas, breaks cycles of envy, and dispels obsessive influences. It is no coincidence that many also use it in baths and amulets, but in smudging, its strength becomes airborne, penetrating every corner, even the most hidden.

Guinea-hen weed is a plant of confrontation. Its vibration is electric, cutting, precise. Used in smudging aimed at direct combat against opposing forces, it is common in works of *descarrego* (spiritual cleansing), protection, and expulsion of entities refusing to leave the environment. Its use, however, demands respect, for just as it repels evil, it can also disturb those whose vibration is misaligned. Guinea-hen weed tolerates no dissimulation. It reveals. And therefore, its smoke, besides cleansing, also exposes.

Rosemary and lavender, on the other hand, are herbs of balance and elevation. While the former act as warriors, these work as harmonizers. When burned, they bring peace, calm, mental clarity, favoring communication with spiritual guides and entities of light. After heavy smudging, it is common to use rosemary or lavender to soften the field and restore lightness to the environment.

Sacred resins, such as myrrh, incense, and frankincense, also hold a prominent place. These substances, extracted from ancient trees, have been used for millennia in rituals of various cultures. Myrrh is known for its ability to deeply cleanse the spiritual environment and facilitate connection with the divine. Frankincense is associated with angelic presence, widely used in Christian ceremonies, especially in Orthodox and Catholic churches. The smoke emanating from it creates a bridge between the altar and the heavens, making the space worthy of receiving the sacred.

In the esoteric rites of the Western tradition, smudging is also a common practice. Hermetic schools, initiatic orders, and practitioners of high magic use specific incenses for each type of magical operation. Sulfur, for example, is used for powerful banishments. Storax, for consecrations. Camphor, for intense cleansing. Each aroma, each density of smoke, each color of the ember reveals the nature of the work. Nothing is done by chance. The invisible world responds to codes, and aromas are one of them.

The way smudging is conducted is as important as the elements used. In many traditions, it is done clockwise—to attract beneficial forces—or counterclockwise—to expel. The practitioner walks firmly through the rooms, chanting prayers, mantras, or songs, guiding the smoke with a fan, a feather, or their own hand. Intention, as always, drives the action. If the person is distracted, fearful, or doubtful, the smoke dissipates without strength. But if they impose themselves with awareness and faith, each spiral of smoke becomes an invisible blade, cutting the bonds of evil.

There is also the custom of smudging one's own body. Passing the body through the smoke is an act of energetic realignment. The head, shoulders, heart, feet—each part of the body receives the plant's vibration, absorbing what is lacking and releasing what is surplus. In cases of great spiritual burden, it is common for the person to feel dizzy, yawn, tear up, or even cry during smudging. This is not fragility; it is a sign of release.

The smoke does what needs to be done, even if the mind does not understand.

In modern times, many reduce smudging to a decorative gesture, perfuming the house with market incense. But the true power lies not in the pleasant smell, but in the consciousness with which it is burned. Incense lit for aesthetics is just an aroma. But when lit with intention, invocation, and respect, it becomes an instrument of power. True smudging is a rite, and every rite requires presence.

It is important to note that some spiritual entities cannot tolerate certain aromas. There are reports in various traditions of spirits immediately withdrawing when exposed to the smoke of certain herbs. But there are also those who draw near. Therefore, knowing what is being burned and why is fundamental. Smudging is not a game. It is a silent conversation with the spiritual world. And like any conversation, it requires listening as much as speaking.

The wisdom contained in the practice of smudging spans the ages like an ember that never goes out, lit by wise hands and awakened hearts. What burns in the embers is not just the herb, but the old within us—that which has stagnated, needs purification, renaming, or dissolution. The smoke, in this process, is both bridge and mirror: it rises to the heavens with the practitioner's intentions, but also returns, enveloping them in a veil that reveals the state of their soul. Therefore, smudging is not merely an external ritual—it is an act of listening, a sensitive communion with the invisible essence of things. When conducted with reverence, it not only cleanses but teaches.

Each culture has shaped this knowledge in its own way, but in all, it maintains the same guiding thread: transforming space so the sacred can inhabit it. In today's world, where mental noise, constant stimuli, and emotional tensions imbalance the vibrational field, smudging re-emerges as a precious resource, not only for protection but for reconnection. It realigns the practitioner with the subtler rhythms of nature, restores the home to its role as a temple, and reminds the body that it too is an altar. Even in silence, smoke speaks—and he who learns to read its spirals begins to perceive the signs of a universe that has never stopped responding.

In the end, smudging is an act of courage: lighting the fire with intention, offering to the flame what no longer serves, and allowing the smoke to carry away the veils obscuring the spirit. It is remembering that there is living intelligence in plants, an ancient language in aromas, and sacredness in the simple act of walking with an incenser in hand and faith in the heart. Because when the smoke rises, something in us also elevates.

Chapter 8
Shield Meditation

The mind, when pacified, becomes armor. The spirit, when centered, becomes a fortress. And between the veils of the visible and invisible, there is an ancestral practice quietly traversing traditions, uniting monks, masters, and initiates under a common understanding: spiritual reality is moldable by consciousness, and consciousness can be trained to erect defenses that no shadow can penetrate. It is in this subtle space of inner mastery that shield meditation is born—a practice transforming the aura into a bastion, thought into a sword, and intention into a seal.

This technique, more than visualization, is alchemy of perception. By forming a shield through meditation, the practitioner does not create something illusory, but organizes the layers of their energy field into vibrational patterns that repel all dissonant frequencies. The mind, far from being an ungoverned stage of impulses, becomes the architect of its own spiritual security. There is no fantasy here. There is construction. There is subtle engineering. And when executed with discipline, shield meditation transforms into a real field, perceptible even by those who do not understand its origin.

Tibetan Buddhist traditions offer some of the most refined examples of this practice. In many monasteries, young monks are taught to form mental fields around their bodies even before beginning advanced enlightenment practices. They visualize lights, protective deities, mandalas spinning around them, flaming seals, and walls of luminous nectar. Every detail is sustained by hours of concentration. In the end, not only does the mind quiet—the entire being vibrates at another frequency, impenetrable to intrusive thoughts, wandering entities, or external influences.

In Reiki, especially in its deeper variations like Tibetan Reiki and Karuna Reiki, energetic protection is built through mentally activated symbols. The practitioner mentally draws the sacred seals, which act as dimensional keys. Each symbol, visualized with pure intention, manifests in the auric field, creating layers of light that repel any attempt at energetic invasion. The aura illuminates, closes, seals. And more than that: it responds with spiritual intelligence.

Western esoteric schools, such as Rosicrucianism, Theosophy, and Ceremonial Magic, also approach protective meditation as a fundamental tool. In many of these paths, the student is guided to create geometric structures around their own body—octahedrons, spheres, inverted pyramids—made of light or subtle matter, each corresponding to a specific element or frequency. These shapes are not inventions, but real structures on the astral plane. And, once repeatedly activated, they become permanent, always ready to be reinforced or updated.

But how is this shield built? The technique varies by spiritual school, but the principles remain: focus, breath, intention, visualization, and repetition. The following practice is a safe synthesis, widely recognized by various traditions:

First, the practitioner should sit with an erect spine, preferably in a quiet place where they will not be disturbed. The eyes can be closed or half-closed. Breathing is the entry point. Inhale deeply through the nose, hold the air for a few seconds, and exhale slowly through the mouth. Repeat this cycle until the mind enters a state of lightness and attention.

With breathing stabilized, focus turns to the center of the chest—the heart chakra. Visualize a small sphere of light there, the size of a pearl. This light can be white, golden, or blue, according to the practitioner's intuition. It pulses, as if breathing with the body. With each inhalation, this sphere grows. With each exhalation, it expands.

In a few minutes, this sphere encompasses the entire body, enveloping every cell. Then, it overflows, forming a cocoon of light around the body. This cocoon is the shield. But it is not static. It spins, pulses, responds. By visualizing it spinning slowly clockwise, the practitioner fully activates it. Symbols like crosses, six-pointed stars, protective eyes, or mantras floating in the energy field can be added to the visualization.

During this process, it is crucial to maintain a firm intention: "Nothing that does not come from light is permitted to enter." This phrase, spoken mentally, acts as vibrational programming. The shield feeds on intention. It is not unbreakable on its own. Its strength lies in the clarity of the mind sustaining it.

Practiced daily, this exercise strengthens the subtle bodies. It is not uncommon for the practitioner, over time, to notice changes in their surroundings: toxic people naturally distance themselves, previously oppressive environments become neutral, psychic attacks lose strength before reaching them. This is not coincidence—it is active protection at work.

There are also more advanced variations. Some traditions teach anchoring the shield with the four elements. Visualize, for example, a flame burning at the four corners of the field, or a circle of water spinning at high speed around the body. Others involve invoking spiritual guides, guardian angels, or warrior archetypes, such as Archangel Michael, Durga, or Ogum. These beings not only protect—they teach. They strengthen the practitioner's psychic structure, so they learn to sustain their own field without eternally depending on external forces.

Shield meditation can also be applied to environments. A room, a house, a vehicle, even an object can be energetically sealed using this technique. Visualize the space being filled with light, all energetic exits being sealed, and a symbolic seal being placed at the central point. This seal can be mental or physical—a drawing made with salt, a consecrated candle, a crystal. The important thing is that it represents the decision to make that place sacred, free from interference.

It is necessary to emphasize that this type of protection does not replace an ethical life. A powerful mental shield can block external attacks, but it does not protect against internal cracks caused by lies, addictions, malice, or constant emotional imbalance. Shield meditation is a tool on a larger path, requiring integrity and continuous evolution.

It is also common, after frequent use of this practice, for the practitioner to notice when their shield is weakened. Sensations of sudden irritation, headaches without physical cause, extreme fatigue after social interactions are indicators that the field has been violated or is draining energy. In these moments, one does not panic—one returns to the base. Sit, breathe, visualize, and rebuild the field calmly. The practice restores control.

It is in this constant return to the base that true mastery reveals itself. The practitioner learns that protecting oneself is not an act of isolation, but of presence. Shield meditation does not erect walls against the world, but delineates vibrational boundaries where the sacred can flourish safely. By reinforcing this practice with consistency and respect, the person develops not only a robust energy field but also a new perspective on themselves: more lucid, firmer, less reactive. And in this state of lucidity, it becomes harder to be manipulated by external forces, whether subtle or visible, as the spirit finds its center—and remains there.

There is a silent nobility in this daily cultivation. Contrary to what many imagine, true spiritual protection does not translate into opaque, rigid shields, but into living, dynamic, attentive fields. The light radiating from an aligned heart, focused mind, and awakened soul is, in itself, an invitation to order. And at the same time, a warning to those vibrating dissonantly: here, there are no breaches.

Shield meditation, when deeply understood, reveals itself as a pedagogy of care—not just care for one's own field, but for the frequency emitted into the world, for everything built within reverberates without. Over time, the shield ceases to be just a technique and becomes an extension of the self. With each conscious breath, each thought aligned with light, the field renews. With each challenge faced with balance, it strengthens. And thus, the shield is no longer something visualized—it is something one is. A firm presence in the invisible, a quiet strength that protects without oppressing, repels without confronting, illuminates without exhausting. In this state, the practitioner not only walks protected—they walk as living protection.

Chapter 9
Ritualistic Baths

When skin feels water, the spirit responds. And it is not just the temperature or the liquid touch that soothes—it is the mystery it carries within. Water, in its deepest essence, is one of the greatest energy conductors Earth knows. In every drop, there is memory, vibration, movement, healing. But it is when united with herbs, salts, prayers, and intention that it transcends its physical function and transforms into a sacred instrument. The ritualistic bath, present in multiple spiritual traditions, is one of the oldest acts of purification, *descarrego* (cleansing), and protection. There is no true religion without some rite involving water at its core. There is no ancestral culture that did not intuitively understand that the body accumulates what does not belong to it, and that the soul sometimes needs washing with more than silence. In baths prepared wisely, herbs speak, elements awaken, and spirits bow. They do not just cleanse: they dissolve, break, liberate.

In the Wiccan tradition, baths are moments of deep communion with nature. Witches understand that each plant possesses a spirit, a unique vibration responding to distinct purposes. A bath with lavender does not have the same effect as one with rosemary. The former brings tranquility, elevates emotional frequency, and facilitates contact with spiritual guides. The latter, meanwhile, is solar, active, wards off astral larvae and stagnant vibrations. When the power of salts—especially sea salts—is added to these ingredients, a powerful solution is created to break invisible blockages.

Baths, in these contexts, are prepared with respect. Leaves are not thrown in haphazardly, nor are components mixed without criteria. Each element is selected according to the lunar phase, the ritual's purpose, and the person's energetic need. A cleansing bath requires cutting herbs: rue, guinea-hen weed, sword-of-saint-george. An attraction bath requires sweet herbs: basil, cinnamon, white rose, chamomile. And there are also sealing baths, using balancing herbs like lavender, rosemary, and anise.

In traditions of African origin, like Quimbanda, Umbanda, and Candomblé, baths are part of the adept's spiritual foundation. They are not optional. They are spiritual prescriptions received through oracles, like cowrie shell divination or consultation with guides. When a person goes through a certain situation—a spiritual attack, deep sadness, an energetic demand—they receive guidance to take a specific "herb bath." These baths are called "cleansing baths," "purification baths," "path-opening baths," among others.

Preparation follows a strict protocol. Leaves should preferably be harvested in a moment of silence and connection. Many spiritual houses teach asking the plant's permission before picking it, recognizing its consciousness. Then, the herbs are manually macerated with room-temperature water, releasing their oils, life energy, *axé*. The mixture is then strained and set aside. Next, the bath is taken from the neck down, while reciting an appropriate prayer or chant. The body is not rinsed afterward—it dries naturally, allowing the plants' energy to fixate in the aura.

There are baths made with denser elements, like vinegar, powdered charcoal, alcohol, pepper, and even gunpowder. These are breaking baths—used only in extreme cases, where witchcraft is active, very dense obsessors are present, or spiritual burdens do not dissolve with gentle herbs. They are risky baths, usually done under the guidance of guides or priests, as they can provoke intense physical and emotional reactions. They are not recreational, not experimental. They are bitter spiritual remedies that should only be used when all other options have failed.

In Hoodoo, an African American spiritual practice blending folk Christianity, root medicine, and African-derived magic, baths have a similar connotation but with unique elements. Preparation includes coarse salt, ammonia, lemon, apple cider vinegar, dried herbs, and prayers. Baths are taken sequentially—for seven days, three days, or according to the necessary symbolic number—and the bathwater is not discarded arbitrarily. Often, it is recommended to throw it outside the house, far from the entrance, or at crossroads, to seal the cleansing.

In all these systems, the bath is more than cleansing: it is a rite of rebirth. The person entering the bath is not the same as the one leaving. Something detaches. Something reorganizes. Something is returned to the earth, the wind, time. And that something, often, is what was preventing true protection from taking hold. Because one does not protect what is still contaminated—one protects what has already been cleaned, restored, remade.

Therefore, ritualistic baths are also used as preparation for other rituals. Before lighting a candle for an angel, before entering a magic circle, before offering a deeper prayer, it is common for the practitioner to take a bath. It is not merely symbolic. It adjusts the frequency. Water, running down the skin, carries away mental noise, emotional larvae, invisible interference. And when done with intention, the effect is potentiated.

But baths can also be sabotaged by unconscious habits. After a cleansing bath, one should not immediately return to routine. Ideally, remain silent for a few minutes, wear light-colored clothes, avoid crowds or dense conversations. Often, a person cleanses themselves and, moments later, reconnects with the same influences. Therefore, the bath must be followed by vigilance. It is like surgery: the body was opened, something was removed, and now time is needed to heal.

Besides herbs, many baths use energized crystals, flower essences, consecrated oils, and even prayers written on paper dissolved in water. There are records of magicians writing an adversary's name on paper, immersing it in water with salt and herbs, and offering prayers of liberation, returning to the universe everything sent to them. It is not a revenge spell—it is vibrational restitution. What is mine returns to me. What is yours returns to you.

Baths with white rose petals and honey, for example, are classics for attracting peace, love, and emotional protection. Baths with bay leaves, cloves, and cinnamon act as financial shielding and opening of material paths. And there are silent baths, where no word is spoken. The practitioner simply enters the water and allows it to speak, touch, teach. Because water has memory. And it knows how to teach.

Some practices recommend taking the bath during the correct moon phase. Waning moon for cleansing. Waxing moon for attraction. Full moon for power and expansion. New moon for starting something anew. Observing these cycles respects the cosmic dance. It recognizes that even water has its time. And that each bath is a dialogue between the body and time.

And it is precisely in this dialogue between body and time that the ritualistic bath reveals its most hidden depth. Each gesture—from harvesting the herb to the last drop of water running down the skin—carries a coded intention, a silent prayer resonating on invisible planes. The act of bathing then becomes a ceremony of return: to essence, balance, inner clarity. Water not only cleanses, it restarts. And when this restart is done with reverence, the soul responds with lightness, as if reminded of its true nature.

This is also why so many spiritual masters emphasize the importance of regular baths in journeys of self-knowledge. It is not about superstition or ritualistic automatism, but vibrational refinement. A well-cared-for energy field not only repels what is harmful—it attracts what is elevated. The person cultivating this practice begins to walk with a different frequency, less susceptible to daily wear, more attentive to their own cycles, more available to the sacred. And this transformation, though subtle to external eyes, translates into synchronicities, emotional healings, and keener intuition when facing life's challenges.

Deep down, every ritual bath is an invitation to silence and listening. An invitation for water to tell us, with its liquid and ancestral language, what we forget in the day's rush, the world's excesses, the mind's shadows. It asks only for presence—and, in return, delivers purification, protection, and reconnection. Therefore, more than a technique, the bath is a living reminder that the sacred dwells in details, and that even the simplest act, when done with soul, has the power to transform.

Chapter 10
Ancestors and Guides

There is a memory that does not fade, even when the name is forgotten. It walks silently beneath our feet, whispers in our ears as we sleep, and manifests in the deepest instincts. This memory has a face, blood, and spirit. They are the ancestors—those who came before, who paved the way with firm or hesitant steps, but always with the strength that crosses generations. In many spiritual traditions, the link with ancestors is not just genealogical remembrance: it is a source of power, protection, guidance. To deny ancestors is like cutting a tree's roots. To honor them is to erect an invisible fortress around the soul.

Ancestor worship is as old as fire. Before temples, before organized religions, there was respect for the dead. They were not seen as absent, but as present on another plane, attentive to the fate of the living. In times of crisis, their names were invoked. In moments of healing, their counsel was heard. Altars, made of stones, bones, or simple offerings, served only this function: keeping the channel open between those who departed and those who remained. Because, deep down, no one truly leaves. Blood remembers. The soul recognizes.

In Kardecist Spiritism, the presence of spiritual guides and ancestors is a fundamental part of understanding life beyond the veil. Allan Kardec, codifying the doctrine's principles, established that the spirits of the departed continue to accompany the living, influencing their decisions, protecting or warning according to vibrational affinity. The protector spirit, also called guardian angel or guide, is a being who chose to accompany a specific individual throughout their incarnate life. They do not interfere with free will but suggest, inspire, protect against major falls, and support in inevitable pains. These guides were not always relatives. Many are souls who have already lived on Earth, evolved, and now undertake missions of accompaniment. But among the guides, there are also direct ancestors—grandparents, great-grandparents, great-great-grandparents—who, through soul affinity or karmic responsibility, remain with the clan. These spirits know. They see. They know the root of problems that seem new today but merely repeat unresolved patterns.

In African traditions, especially those of Yoruba origin like Candomblé, ancestors are called eguns. They have their own cults, sacred spaces, specific rites. One of the best known is the Egungun cult, where the spirits of the dead manifest through dances, colorful clothing, and ritualized movements. These are not casual evocations—they are reunions with the community's memory. Eguns are honored, respected, and, in many cases, feared. For the ancestor is not always benevolent. They bring justice, balance the clan's spiritual accounts, and can both protect and correct.

In Umbanda, spiritual guides present themselves in lines of work: *caboclos* (indigenous spirits), *pretos-velhos* (spirits of enslaved elders), *crianças* (child spirits), *boiadeiros* (cowboy spirits), *marinheiros* (sailor spirits). Each line possesses a specific vibration and fulfills a function within the consultee's journey. *Caboclos*, for example, are spirits of indigenous warriors bringing strength, courage, firmness. *Pretos-velhos* are spirits of formerly enslaved people, bearers of ancestral wisdom, patience, and healing power. These are not symbolic roles—they are living consciousnesses, with history, personality, and defined mission. When incorporated by mediums in sessions, they act as channels for protection, cleansing, guidance, and rebalancing.

But one need not be a medium to connect with a guide. The link can be made through sincere prayer, a written letter, a thought repeated with intention. The guide hears. The ancestor responds. It might be through a dream, a sudden intuition, an unexpected sign. Those who have learned to silence the mind's noise know how to recognize these signs. A feather on the path, an old song, a scent from nowhere—these are marks left by those who no longer have voice, but still have presence.

In Shinto, the ancestral religion of Japan, ancestors are literally deified. Each home has a *kamidana*, an altar where incense, flowers, food, and prayers are offered to the family spirits. These spirits, called "kami," protect the lineage, influence births, marriages, harvests. They are treated with profound respect, and their wishes are considered in important decisions. Worship of the dead is not seen as morbid, but as part of the ethics of living. Forgetting those who came before means losing direction in the present.

Spiritual guides also manifest in higher forms in some traditions, not just as spirits of individuals, but as collective intelligences. Archangels, ascended masters, interdimensional entities—these higher forms of consciousness act as guides for collectives, nations, or spiritual groups. Some see them as myths. Others feel them as vibrational realities as intense as their own body. What matters is not the label, but the result: these beings work for the evolution of consciousness and offer protection to those who tune into their vibration.

Connection with ancestors and guides can be strengthened through simple and powerful practices. Maintaining an altar, even a discreet one, is one of the most effective gestures. On it, photos, symbolic objects, candles, a glass of water, fresh flowers can be placed. This space becomes a vibrational anchor point, a place where veils thin and communication intensifies. There one talks, gives thanks, asks, cries. And there, often, one hears the answer that would not come otherwise.

Another fundamental practice is gratitude. Thanking ancestors and guides not just for favors, but for their mere presence, strengthens the spiritual bond. Gratitude is a vibrational field that amplifies natural protection. When the spirit feels recognized, it responds vigorously. The remembered guide walks closer. The honored ancestor remains vigilant. Forgetfulness weakens. Recognition strengthens.

There is also the importance of silence. Many signs are missed because the mind is too noisy. Guides speak in whispers. Ancestors manifest in echoes. Only those who withdraw inward can hear them. Meditation, intuitive writing, lucid dreams are doors that open to this communication. And once opened, they do not close easily. The flow becomes constant. The spiritual field adjusts. The soul feels less alone.

It is not uncommon for a guide's protection to prevent accidents, divert dangerous paths, undo enchantments. Countless reports exist of people who, upon lighting a candle for their protector, felt an inexplicable wave of peace. Others who, after dreaming of a deceased relative, awoke healed from old emotional pains. Some who, following an intuition from nowhere, escaped tragedies. This is not superstition. It is attunement.

But it is necessary to remember that guides are not servants. They do not act on demand, nor respond to whims. They see further. What we ask for may not be what we need. What we desire may harm us. And therefore, often, their silence is protection. The absence of response is also a response. Because their mission is evolution, not comfort.

Finally, the link with ancestors and guides is a two-way street. Just as they protect us, we also feed them with our gestures, our light, our choices. When a descendant heals an old pain, they liberate an ancestor who carried that guilt. When a child breaks a toxic pattern, they honor those who came before and pave the way for those who will come. Spiritual protection, in this sense, is a chain linking past, present, and future—and the strongest link is always forged in love.

It is in this love that the bond with ancestors and guides takes root most firmly. It is not distant devotion, but a living alliance, nurtured by listening, reverence, and commitment to one's own evolution. When a person recognizes themselves as part of a spiritual lineage—be it familial, cultural, or universal—they cease to walk alone. There is a chorus of voices behind each step, an ancient breath sustaining the decisions of now. And it is this recognition that strengthens the field, making the being less vulnerable to deviations and more attuned to what truly matters.

Over time, this presence becomes as familiar as thought itself. Guides cease to be ethereal figures and become intimate counselors. Ancestors, previously remembered only on specific dates, come to live in small daily choices, in maintained values, in gestures repeated without knowing why. It is as if, by honoring the invisible, the visible aligns. Life becomes more fluid, cycles more understandable, challenges less solitary. After all, no one walks forsaken when they have an altar lit within. And often, this altar reveals itself in the form of accurate intuitions, transformative encounters, or signs arriving as if already known.

Thus, keeping the relationship with ancestors and guides alive is more than a spiritual ritual—it is a way of living with deep roots and eyes open to the heavens. It is accepting that we are in the middle of a sacred current, and that every gesture, thought, or word reverberates both backward and forward. And when this awareness takes hold, protection comes not only from outside: it is born from within, sustained by who we were, who we are, and by all who silently walk with us between worlds.

Chapter 11
Lunar Rituals

The moon, with its silent and ever-changing presence, has always held a deep fascination for the human spirit. Its cycle, as subtle as it is precise, shapes the tides, births, feminine cycles, dreams. But there is something beyond biology and physics. There is a hidden language in its pale light, an invisible influence that dances in the shadows and masterfully guides the unseen. Since the dawn of time, ancient peoples realized the moon not only illuminates the night—it reveals portals, amplifies intentions, dispels spells, and summons ancestral forces. Lunar rituals, therefore, are bridges between the visible and the hidden, between the now and the eternal.

At the heart of the oldest spiritual traditions, the moon was regarded as a goddess. The Great Mother, the Lady of Mysteries, the Queen of the Night. In its cycle of birth, growth, fullness, and death, it reflected the cycle of life and spirit. Each lunar phase possesses a distinct frequency, a unique vibrational field that can be harnessed for specific purposes. Understanding this cycle means recognizing that time is not linear—it is spiral, symbolic, full of subtle layers.

The new moon is the point of germination. It is the dark womb of time, the moment where nothing is seen, but everything is prepared. At this point in the cycle, rituals are focused on silence, retreat, introspection. It is time to plant intentions, write desires, set goals. There is no harvest yet—only sowing. Candles used in this phase are usually black, dark blue, or purple, representing mystery, protection, and connection with the invisible. The altar may be adorned with stones like obsidian, onyx, or amethyst. Prayers are directed towards the hidden aspects of the self, asking for clarity of spiritual vision and protection on the paths yet to be trodden.

In the waxing phase, energy rises. The moon shows itself as a crescent, pointing upwards, like an ascending smile in the sky. It is the time for movement, for putting into practice what was desired. Rituals of attraction, strengthening, growth, and path-opening are especially potent during this period. Green or golden candles are lit. Rosemary oil, bay leaves, sunflower seeds are used. Prosperity baths, smudging to accelerate projects, and prayers directed at strengthening willpower are common. The energy of the waxing moon is electric, expansive, conducive to pacts with the future.

The full moon is the queen on her throne. Her total light fills the night, and her vibrational field reaches its peak. It is in this phase that portals open most easily. The veil between worlds becomes thinner, and entities—both beneficial and hostile—circulate with greater intensity. Full moon rituals are the most powerful. Any intention set during this phase will be amplified. It is the time for consecrations, celebrations with nature, invocations to lunar deities like Hecate, Isis, Diana, or Yemanjá. White candles, myrrh incense, white flowers, and cups of water are offered as symbols of purity and fullness.

During the full moon, many traditions practice "charging" crystals, amulets, magical instruments, and even water. Leaving these objects under the moonlight is a way to bathe them in pure, vibrant energy. Lunar water, for example, is prepared by placing a jar or bowl of water under the full moonlight throughout the night. In the morning, this water can be used in baths, sprinkled in environments, or added to other rituals. It carries the energy of the peak, revelation, clarity, and power.

But not all light is benign. The fullness of the moon also reveals what is hidden. Many spiritual attacks occur under the full moon, as it potentiates not only the good but everything latent. Therefore, protection rituals are essential in this phase. Casting magic circles, using sealing crystals like black tourmaline or hematite, and maintaining constant prayers are recommended practices to avoid invasions during this period.

The waning moon brings the time for release. The light begins to recede, and with it go masks, excesses, illusions. It is time for banishment, deep healing, closure. Rituals of this phase are aimed at cutting off what sickens: toxic relationships, destructive habits, negative spiritual ties. Coarse salt, activated charcoal, rue leaves, vinegar, and pepper are used. Black or brown candles are lit. Words gain cutting power. Prayers, when made truthfully, dissolve old bonds and free the soul to begin anew. It is common, in waning moon rituals, to write on pieces of paper everything one wishes to remove: fears, sorrows, illnesses, addictions. These papers are then burned in a small cauldron or buried far from home, symbolizing the surrender to the earth of what no longer serves. The smoke carries it aloft. The ash returns it to the Earth's womb. And the spirit breathes lighter.

Kabbalistic astrology offers an even deeper layer of understanding regarding lunar rituals. Each lunar month has a specific rulership, associated with one of the twelve tribes of Israel, a zodiac sign, and a spiritual challenge. Celebrating the new moon (Rosh Chodesh) according to this system means aligning with the purpose of that cycle, opening up to karmic healing, and attuning to the celestial codes governing creation. Prayers are based on psalms, Kabbalistic divine names, and symbols of the Tree of Life. Each moon offers a chance to reprogram the soul.

In modern witchcraft, especially Wicca, the Esbat—celebration of the full moon—is considered one of the most important rites. Held outdoors whenever possible, it gathers practitioners in magic circles, with chants, dances, spells, and offerings. The goddess is invoked under different names, and the elements are called to form a sacred field of power. The energy generated in these gatherings not only protects participants but expands its influence to the entire community. These are moments of great elevation and spiritual strengthening.

However, it is fundamental for the practitioner to understand that the lunar ritual is not just a performance. It is a mirror. The moon reflects the internal state of the one invoking it. If there is confusion, the ritual will bring difficult revelations. If there is purity, it will amplify the light. The moon does not deceive—it merely exposes. Therefore, before performing any practice under its governance, a brief examination of conscience is necessary. Know what is sought, recognize what is carried, accept what needs transmutation.

Many practitioners keep a lunar journal. In it, they note their experiences during each phase, recurring dreams, emotional changes, practices performed, and perceived results. This record creates a deeper bond with the moon and allows the practitioner to perceive patterns, understand their own cycles, and refine their attunement to spiritual time. The moon passes, but leaves signs. And those who note them learn to read these signs more clearly.

The moon teaches that nothing is static. Everything grows, overflows, recedes, and dies—only to be reborn. Lunar rituals, when practiced consciously, align the being with this cosmic dance. They do not serve to force destiny, but to teach the right time to act, wait, let go. And therein lies their greatest power: making the practitioner not a manipulator of forces, but an ally of universal order.

The connection with the moon is, therefore, a two-way street—a call and response between the visible and the invisible. By following its rhythms, the practitioner not only harmonizes their intentions with natural cycles but also learns to listen more deeply to themselves. Each ritual is not an end in itself, but an intimate conversation with existence, where nature answers questions the intellect cannot formulate. The discipline of tracking lunar phases becomes, over time, a refined form of self-knowledge, where each offering, each prayer, each silence carries a symbolic weight surpassing matter.

Furthermore, the regular practice of these rituals creates a kind of energy field extending beyond the individual. Homes become spiritually cleaner, relationships rebalance, previously cloudy paths begin to clear. The moon, with its reflected light, shows that one need not shine by oneself to influence profoundly. So too is inner work: silent, constant, yet capable of generating immense transformations.

By integrating lunar rituals into daily life, the practitioner develops heightened sensitivity, perceiving that every detail of the universe is an instruction, a symbol, a revelation awaiting attention. In the end, the true lunar alchemy happens not on altars or in ceremonies, but within the observer. It is there that the seed cast on the new moon germinates, grows, blossoms, and fades. The cycle demands not control, but surrender. And he who accepts dancing to the moon's rhythm ultimately discovers that true power lies in allowing the soul to move with the cosmos, without resistance—only presence.

Chapter 12
Exu and Guardians

Where does fear end and respect begin? Where does prejudice dissolve and mystery reveal itself? In many paths of Brazilian spirituality, this boundary point manifests in the name of Exu—guardian entity, messenger, lord of the crossroads, bearer of secrets and keys. Misunderstood for centuries, defamed by ignorance, and distorted by dogmas, Exu did not bow. He remained, firm at the crossroads, at the portals between worlds, at the forefront of rituals, at the feet of mediums, and in the breath of those who carry consciousness. Because Exu is a guardian. And a guardian does not ask permission: he protects.

Exu is not the devil. Exu is not a demon. These ideas, planted in bad faith by colonizing religious structures, tried to erase ancestral wisdom that resisted pain, slavery, and marginalization. Exu is a cosmic force acting as an interface between planes. In Umbanda, he is a spirit who has lived, knows humans in their depth, and chose to work on the left-hand path—not because he is evil, but because he deals with liminal zones, boundaries, with what is clean and also with what needs cleaning.

In Quimbanda, Exu assumes an even more complex and powerful position. There, he is treated with firmness, respect, and precision. The Exus of Quimbanda are not vague spirits: they are entities with names, characteristics, histories, specific chants (*pontos cantados*), and rituals. Exu Tranca-Ruas, Exu Caveira, Exu Marabô, Exu Veludo, Exu Sete Encruzilhadas—each operates in a distinct vibrational range, offering protection, cutting demands, opening paths, judgment, and spiritual justice. They are soldiers of the astral, walking between worlds, facing what many dare not look at.

Pomba Gira, in turn, is the lady of feminine force in Exu's line. She is not a prostitute, as popular distortion tries to suggest. She is the lady of sacred sensuality, magnetism, the force of creation and destruction. She deals with desire, emotional bonds, pacts of the heart. She also acts as a guardian, breaking destructive bonds, restoring autonomy to the body, sovereignty to the soul. Pomba Gira Rainha, Cigana das Almas, Maria Padilha, Rosa Caveira—all are manifestations of this archetype of spiritual power that protects with eyes seeing what love hides.

Exu's role as a spiritual guardian extends beyond the individual. He is the guardian of the house, the *terreiro* (spiritual center), the portals between planes. No spiritual work begins without saluting Exu. He owns the portal. He authorizes or denies the passage of entities. He maintains the balance between the visible and invisible. When respected, he protects with unwavering fidelity. When invoked without understanding, he can respond harshly—not out of malice, but justice. He demands truth. And tolerates no hypocrisy.

One pillar of the relationship with Exu is offering. Offerings, for Exu, are not payment—they are recognition. A glass of cachaça, a cigar, a piece of meat, a *padê* made with dendê oil, a red liqueur, seven coins, a *ponto-riscado* on the ground: these are material signs anchoring his energy on the physical plane. Each Exu has specific preferences, which must be known and respected. Offerings are made in places of power—crossroads, cemeteries, railway lines, forest entrances—always with due permission and proper guidance. One does not offer out of curiosity. One offers out of alliance.

The ethics of pacts with Exu are clear. He is not a servant, not a magical object, not a guarantee of results. He is an ally. And like any ally, must be treated honestly. Pacts with Exu are vibrational seals: once made, they must be fulfilled. Asking Exu for protection requires reciprocity. He helps, but also teaches. He cuts demands, but also shows the origin of errors. It is common that, after working with Exu, a person goes through events that seem chaotic—but are actually cleansings. Exu removes what is rotten, even if disguised as comfort.

The protection offered by Exu is active. He does not wait for the attack: he watches, patrols, anticipates. Many report dreams with Exu, subtle warnings, premonitions, heightened intuitions. He manifests through signs: an animal crossing the path, a strong smell out of nowhere, a metallic sound, a sudden mood change. Exu does not hide. He marks his presence. And his presence, when welcomed with respect, transforms the protected one's life. Nothing goes unnoticed. No spiritual arrow hits a body walking with Exu ahead.

But the cult of Exu requires courage. Courage to abandon inherited paradigms, learned fears, ingrained prejudices. Exu does not operate where there is falsehood. He unmasks. And this, for many, is painful. Therefore, only those who accept truth as the path remain by his side. He does not demand perfection—he demands authenticity. And in authenticity lies the most powerful shield: the whole being, without masks, without disguises, without guilt.

Symbolically, Exu represents the very axis of being. The meeting point between desires and limits, between the sacred and profane, between heaven and earth. His trident is not a weapon of war—it is a tool of balance. One point aims up, one down, and one forward. It is the integration of worlds. Exu teaches that evil is not fought with denial, but with awareness. That one does not flee the shadow—one illuminates it. And that real spiritual protection exists only when facing what is hidden.

It is important to remember that Exu does not walk alone. He operates with legions, lines of work, other spiritual guardians. Many spiritual workers are accompanied by Exus and Pomba Giras who do not manifest publicly but are always present in sessions, behind the scenes, in the silent early mornings when the medium feels the weight of the world. It is these guardians who secure the rear, seal rituals, ward off hostile entities, protect the children of the house even when they forget to ask.

Not infrequently, people suffering severe spiritual attacks only find relief after direct work with Exu. When obsession persists, when negative magic resists, when mental disturbance has no clinical explanation, it is Exu who enters with force. He breaks bonds, collects spirits, dispels spells, closes portals opened by ignorance. But he demands posture. Demands righteousness. Demands decision. Exu does not protect those who hesitate. He protects those who choose.

In the end, walking with Exu means taking ownership of one's destiny. It means stopping blaming others. It means looking at one's own desires and recognizing power in them too. It means building protection not just with candles and offerings, but with attitudes, choices, words, and silences. Exu does not want followers—he wants conscious beings. And alongside the conscious, he builds fortresses that no shadow can penetrate.

Exu is also the master of transitions. Not just physical or spiritual crossroads, but the moments when the soul wavers between fear and courage, doubt and action. His strength manifests the instant the practitioner chooses to stand firm before the unknown and proclaim: "I am here." In this simple act of presence, Exu reveals himself intensely. He does not demand blind faith—he demands experience. And it is in this experience that he teaches that spirituality is not an escape from reality, but a dive into it with open eyes and a firm chest. He does not separate the profane from the sacred: he stitches them together, thread by thread, until life becomes whole.

Alongside Exu, we understand that spiritual protection is not the absence of conflicts, but the ability to traverse them with lucidity. That cleansing is not erasing the past, but reframing it. That strength is not imposition, but true presence. When a spiritual guardian manifests, they do so with the weight of their history, the responsibility of their function, and the freedom of their spirit. Exu does not judge by appearances—he reads intentions. Does not respond to masks—responds to truths. Therefore, his protégés learn, sooner or later, to cultivate clarity as a weapon and humility as a shield.

Walking with Exu is a pact with life as it is: contradictory, rich, unpredictable, sacred. It is accepting that there is no light without shadow, nor healing without confrontation. But it is also knowing that, with Exu ahead, no abyss is an end—it is passage. No locked door is a sentence—it is pause. And no pain is punishment—it is teaching. The guardian of the crossroads does not close trails: he teaches how to open one's own. And by teaching, transforms every human being who allows themselves to walk with him not into a believer, not a servant—but a warrior of their own truth.

Chapter 13
Kabbalah and the Tree of Life

There exists a hidden structure sustaining all creation. An invisible architecture, composed of paths, forces, names, and energies, interconnecting the higher worlds with the lower worlds, offering the human spirit a route of ascent and protection. This structure is called the Tree of Life, belonging to the tradition of Kabbalah—the mystical body of Judaism, which for centuries remained hidden, reserved only for initiates capable of understanding its secrets. But when the soul cries out for deep protection, and common means suffice no longer, it is among the branches of this sacred tree that the oldest seals of spiritual defense are found.

Kabbalah is not a belief system. It is a map. A mirror of the internal and external universe. Each of the ten sefirot—the spheres of the Tree of Life—represents not only a divine aspect but also a stage of the human being. And to protect oneself, in the light of Kabbalah, is to harmonize these spheres within, so that no misdirected force can penetrate the soul's imbalances. For every spiritual breach is, first and foremost, a mismatch between these internal forces.

At the top of the Tree is Keter, the Crown, the emanation closest to Ein Sof—the Infinite—

representing pure will, connection with the absolute source. Descending the Tree is like descending from light to form, spirit to matter, passing through spheres like Chokmah (wisdom), Binah (understanding), Chesed (mercy), down to Malkuth, the Kingdom, where creation manifests in physical totality. But the Tree can also be ascended—and this ascent, when guided by rituals and sacred names, is one of the most powerful ways to seal the spirit against opposing forces.

Protection in Kabbalah begins with the name. The 72 Names of God, encoded from three verses of Exodus (14:19-21), are combinations of three Hebrew letters acting as vibrational keys. Each of these triads represents a specific divine frequency, capable of illuminating, purifying, protecting, healing, and transforming. They are not common magic words—they are sacred formulas that, when chanted or visualized correctly, vibrate on invisible planes and realign the soul with cosmic order.

Among the Names most used for spiritual protection is Mem-He-Shin, corresponding to the energy of neutralizing negativity. Another, Lamed-Aleph-Vav, acts as a shield against external forces. Yud-Lamed-Yud is used to shield the mind against obsessive thoughts and dense influences. These names are not pronounced as read, lacking vowels—they are chanted with breath, focus, visualization. And it is in this state of total presence that the Name activates its field.

Using the Names of God requires reverence. They can be inscribed on parchments, paper seals, used in consecrated amulets, or visualized in guided meditations. Many Kabbalists write them on the skin with disappearing ink, like a temporary seal of light. Others draw them under pillows or on doorposts. The important thing is that their presence is not trivialized. Each Name is a door. And opening doors unprepared can expose one to what is not desired to be seen.

The Tree of Life, in turn, can be used as a protective field when visualized ritually. The practitioner begins by visualizing Malkuth, at the base of the body—usually the feet—as a golden field representing grounding, stability, protection of the physical plane. Then ascends to Yesod, the center of the base of the spine, symbolizing the unconscious, instincts, and sexuality—protecting against vampirism and subtle manipulations. Continues to Hod and Netzach, the hips, dealing with intellect and emotion. Tiferet, in the center of the chest, is the heart—point of balance and spiritual vulnerability. Geburah and Chesed, the shoulders, represent strength and mercy. Binah and Chokmah, the temples—understanding and wisdom. Finally, Keter, at the crown of the head, seals the field with white light. When this visualization is done daily, with appropriate Names activated in each sphere, a complex and refined, almost impenetrable, protective field is created.

Kabbalah also teaches that there are four worlds: Atziluth (the world of emanation), Beriah (creation), Yetzirah (formation), and Assiah (action). These worlds coexist, and the conscious practitioner can align their protection in all of them. For example: a spiritual obsession might be acting in Yetzirah, the world of emotions. A Kabbalistic seal activated in this specific world unties the knot. A curse cast in Assiah, the physical world, can be reversed with spiritually guided material actions—like charity, fasting, or meditation with psalms.

Psalms, indeed, are used within Kabbalah as vibrational formulas of immense power. Each psalm has a number, an activation code, a specific frequency. Psalm 91, already revered by various traditions, is especially potent when chanted with the original Hebrew intonation. Psalm 23, 121, and 27 are other examples of vibrational shields against negative forces. But it is not enough to read mechanically. One must live the psalm. Feel each verse as a decree. As a sword. As a pact.

Within the Tree of Life, there is also the so-called "Path of the Lightning Flash"—a zigzag route connecting the sefirot downwards, reproducing the path of creation. Reversing this path in meditation is a way to ascend spiritually, purifying the soul's layers and closing open breaches. It is an advanced protection technique, used by experienced Kabbalists to restore the energy field after attacks or prolonged spiritual wear.

Kabbalistic sigils, meanwhile, are graphic representations of the Names of God, Angels, and sefirot. They can be engraved on metals, drawn on parchments, carved in wood. When consecrated by prayer, fasting, and intention, they become protective seals accompanying the practitioner. Many Kabbalists carry these seals hidden in their clothes, sewn inside, or hidden under their pillow. Not as magic talismans, but as vibrational reminders of the alliance with the sacred.

Important reminder: Kabbalah does not tolerate ego. Using its secrets for selfish purposes, revenge, or manipulation results in vibrational collapse. The practitioner attempting to use the Tree of Life for domination or prestige gets lost in psychic labyrinths. Protection, in Kabbalah, is a consequence of righteousness. The Names only respond to the sincere soul. The Tree only manifests to the humble seeker. He who walks with arrogance finds distorted mirrors. He who walks with reverence finds portals.

Therefore, the Kabbalistic practice of protection also demands emotional purity. Hatred, fear, envy, pride—all these feelings create cracks in the vibrational field, through which any influence can infiltrate. Before sealing the body with Names or meditations, it is necessary to seal the heart with truth. Inner cleansing is the first shield. Prayer, the second. Discipline, the third. And the Names, finally, merely manifest what already exists within.

The Kabbalistic journey is, above all, a journey of integrity. It is not enough to know the Names, trace the seals, or memorize the paths of the Tree—one must become a mirror of these forces. True protection occurs when the body becomes a temple, the mind aligns with purpose, and the heart vibrates in righteousness. In this state, each sefirah lights up like an internal lamp, illuminating spaces previously occupied by fears or uncertainties. It is in this brightness that the practitioner begins to understand the real meaning of light: not as escape from shadow, but its transcendence.

By working with Kabbalah, the seeker delves into a dimension where language, gesture, intention, and silence intertwine. Nothing is done by chance. A psalm recited purely has more strength than a seal engraved with vanity. A humble visualization can seal more than a hundred names repeated mechanically. Kabbalah teaches that everything is alive: the letter, the sound, the silence between words. And when walking with this respect, the Tree of Life ceases to be an external symbol and begins to blossom within, connecting heaven and earth through existence itself.

Understanding this is the true act of protection. Because he who walks in truth need not hide. He who aligns with the flow need not fight the current. Kabbalah is not just a shield—it is a call. An invitation to refine the soul, to reconcile with the divine dwelling in every cell, every thought, every choice. And he who accepts this call finds not only spiritual security, but a dwelling of silent peace that no evil can traverse.

Chapter 14
Norse Runes

Among the forests of eternal pines, the fjords cutting the land with icy water, and the biting northern winds, ancient wisdom rests in stones. The ancient Norse peoples needed no luxurious temples or sacred books to access the divine. They had the runes. And within them lies not just an alphabet, but a complete system of power, protection, prophecy, and spiritual connection. Runes were not created—they were revealed. And he who carries them with reverence carries invisible shields older than the wars of men.

In Norse tradition, runes are more than letters. Each is a living symbol, a vibrational key, an entity acting on invisible planes. The central myth tells that the god Odin, seeking wisdom, hung himself on the World Tree—Yggdrasil—for nine days and nine nights, wounded, without food or drink, until the runes were revealed to him on the threshold between life and death. He did not learn the runes—he conquered them through sacrifice. Since then, each runic symbol carries this seal of initiation, pain, and truth.

The word "rune" comes from the ancient term meaning "whisper" or "secret." And that is exactly what they are: whispers from the invisible, secrets revealed to those ready to listen. Each rune carries its own vibration, archetype, and active energy. There are 24 symbols in the traditional set known as the Elder Futhark, and each can be used as an instrument of protection when understood, activated, and respected.

Among the runes of greatest protective power is Algiz. Its shape resembles a figure with arms raised, as if invoking the heavens or signaling "stop." It is the rune of defense, the subtle shield, connection with higher forces. When drawn, chanted, or visualized, Algiz creates a field around the practitioner repelling invasive energies, spiritual attacks, and hostile vibrations. Many Viking warriors drew Algiz on their physical shields—but the true shield was spiritual.

Another rune of great strength is Thurisaz, linked to Thor's hammer and the raw power of giants. It is a rune of confrontation, aggressive protection. Its use is not passive—it attacks what threatens. In ritual practices, Thurisaz can be used to cut obsessive ties, undo negative enchantments, and seal open spiritual portals. However, it is a dangerous rune for those who do not master their emotions, as it can reflect anger and impatience if misdirected. Used wisely, it is a sharp sword. Used without control, it can injure the bearer.

Eihwaz, meanwhile, represents the yew tree—sacred tree of the north—and is a symbol of resistance, initiatory death, and psychic protection. It is a silent but profound rune. It acts on the subtlest fields of the mind, strengthening the spiritual field against mental attacks, emotional influences, and energetic vampirism. In meditations, visualizing it at the center of the forehead or base of the spine activates the inner axis, the channel connecting worlds, and seals the body against astral invasions.

Besides individual use, runes can be combined into bindrunes—junctions of two or more symbols to create a specific power seal. For example, uniting Algiz, Eihwaz, and Sowilo (rune of sunlight and victory) forms a protection seal that simultaneously illuminates and repels. These symbols can be drawn on paper, wood, stone, or even visualized around the body. When consecrated with fire, saliva, or blood (depending on the tradition), they become living instruments of defense.

Using runes requires preparation. It is not just about tracing a drawing and expecting results. Runes are entities. They must be awakened with respect. The serious student learns the sound of each rune—as each has a sacred phoneme—and chants this sound as if it were a mantra. This vocalization, known as galdr, activates the rune's vibration on the invisible plane. It is common that, upon chanting a rune with concentration and intention, the practitioner feels immediate changes in the environment: the air thickens, the body tingles, inner vision intensifies.

Runes can also be used in physical talismans. A necklace with Algiz carved in ash wood. A ring with Sowilo engraved in silver. A bracelet with Uruz—the rune of life force—drawn with permanent ink. The material should align with the purpose: wood for earth connection, metal for sealing, stone for durability. These objects must be consecrated with breath, saliva, or fire and kept energetically clean. Upon feeling a talisman is "heavy" or "faded," it should be buried for a night or passed through herb smoke to rebalance.

In many modern rituals inspired by Norse traditions, the magic circle is cast with runes. Each cardinal point receives a specific rune: north, Eihwaz; south, Sowilo; east, Ansuz (divine communication); west, Laguz (intuitive flow). In the center, Mannaz is placed—the rune of the human being, the link between worlds. This circle is not symbolic. It creates an energetic structure organizing space, repelling interference, and anchoring the sacred presence.

Using runes for protection is not limited to the individual. They can be traced on doors, walls, windows, important documents, even electronic devices. In modern times, many digital magicians apply runes to images, passwords, visual codes. But conscious use is essential. A rune is not decoration. It is a contract. And he who traces a contract with the invisible must honor it ethically.

It is important to note that runes respond to blood. This means their action intensifies the more the practitioner commits to truth, integrity, and courage—essential virtues of Norse spirituality. A cowardly heart cannot hold a living rune. A selfish desire breaks the seal. Therefore, before using a protection rune, one must ask oneself: "Am I prepared to carry this energy? Am I willing to honor what it demands?"

Norse tradition teaches that the spiritual warrior wins not by attack, but by clarity. Protection, on this path, is not a wall—it is posture. And runes are tools to awaken this posture. When the practitioner aligns with a rune's truth, they become it. Algiz is not just a drawn symbol—it is a state of consciousness. Thurisaz is not just combat—it is sharp justice. Sowilo is not just light—it is clarity burning away deceit.

Runes also live in dreams. Many apprentices report encounters with runic symbols in night visions, messages left on walls, lights forming in the air, sounds reverberating before waking. These dreams are not mere reveries—they are activations. When a rune appears in a dream, it is introducing itself, offering alliance. It is up to the dreamer to accept it or not. But once accepted, it walks alongside.

This joint walk with the runes transforms the practitioner. They begin to perceive the world not just with eyes, but with a subtler field of perception, where each situation carries a symbol, each encounter reveals a mirror, and each challenge is an invitation to conscious action. Protection, in this context, is no longer an emergency resource, but a continuous state of presence. The rune ceases to be a tool and becomes language—a silent idiom between the visible and invisible, between what manifests and what prepares. That is why, for the ancient Norse, protecting oneself was also honoring one's own destiny.

Over time, the dedicated student realizes they do not choose the runes—the runes choose them. One rune repeats in divination readings. Another appears frequently in dreams. A third reveals itself in moments of silence, when the mind ceases and the spirit listens. This intimate approach creates deep spiritual bonds that cross incarnations. The bond with a rune does not end when a ritual ends—it renews with each ethical gesture, each truth spoken, each step taken firmly. And thus, the practitioner transforms into a guardian of knowledge demanding, above all, responsibility.

The tradition of runes has survived millennia not just for its symbolic beauty—but because it offers, even today, real, living, active protection. It is a legacy that cannot be reduced to aesthetics or superstition. It requires courage, silence, respect. It requires willingness to listen to the ancestral whisper in stones, wind, bones. And he who listens and honors this call begins to tread a path where the shield is internal, combat is lucid, and true power is born not from force, but from the deep alliance between spirit and truth.

Chapter 15
Protective Feng Shui

There are invisible forces traversing our homes like silent winds. They carry intentions, memories, fragments of old emotions, remnants of experiences not belonging to us. An environment can be beautiful to the eyes, yet spiritually harmful. It may seem peaceful on the surface, but contain vibrational cracks through which negativity seeps like smoke. It is at this point that Feng Shui, the ancient Chinese art of harmonizing spaces, reveals itself not as mere aesthetics, but as a powerful tool for spiritual protection.

Feng Shui, literally meaning "wind and water," was born from observing nature's cycles and the relationship between elements and human life. It is not superstition, but a spiritual science understanding that the environment directly influences the flow of Qi—life energy. When Qi flows balanced, life flourishes. When stagnant, it sickens. Feng Shui, in this sense, is medicine for space. And protecting oneself, from its perspective, means transforming the home into a subtle force field, where external influences find no shelter.

The foundation of protective Feng Shui is the bagua—an octagonal energy map dividing space into nine areas corresponding to life aspects: career, wisdom, family, prosperity, fame, relationships, creativity, helpful people, and the center (health and balance). Placing this map over the house plan allows identification of where energies need activation, purification, or sealing. Each bagua area is associated with elements, colors, shapes, and symbols. And each of these associations can be used as a tool to strengthen the environment's vibrational field.

The position of the entrance door is crucial. Energy enters through it. A misaligned, obstructed, or poorly lit door acts as a spiritual bottleneck. Tradition teaches the main entrance should be clean, well-kept, without clutter. Healthy plants, clean mats, wind chimes, well-positioned mirrors, and adequate lighting attract beneficial Qi and prevent negative influences from settling.

One of the most used symbols in protective Feng Shui is the Ba-Gua mirror. It is octagonal, with the yin-yang symbol in the center and the eight trigrams around it. When positioned above the entrance door—outside—it reflects and disperses invasive energies, acting as a vibrational shield. It should not be used inside the house, as its dispersing force can cause internal imbalance. It is a tool of subtle warfare, used only when certain that heavy energies are trying to penetrate the home.

Another essential element in space protection is furniture arrangement. Feng Shui teaches that the position of the bed, desk, and stove determines the energetic security of the inhabitants. The bed should be in a command position: facing the door, but not directly aligned with it. This position allows seeing who enters, keeping the subconscious in a state of safe vigilance. Sleeping with feet pointing directly at the door is considered highly unfavorable, symbolizing spiritual exposure.

The stove, a symbol of prosperity, must be clean, with all burners working, and never positioned directly opposite the sink or refrigerator, as this creates conflict between fire and water elements. When these principles are ignored, the environment vibrates disharmoniously, opening doors to intrigue, financial loss, and emotional instability.

Using crystals is also a powerful practice within Feng Shui. Pyrite, placed in the prosperity area, acts as a shield against scarcity and envy. A multifaceted crystal, hung in windows or dark hallways, refracts light and moves stagnant Qi. Black obsidian, positioned near the entrance or where heavy energy is felt, functions as an absorber and transmuter of dense influences. It is important to regularly cleanse these crystals with water and coarse salt or expose them to sunlight and moonlight to maintain their effectiveness.

Plants, especially those with rounded leaves and vertical growth, are allies in strengthening the house's energy field. Lucky bamboo, snake plant (sword-of-saint-george), and ZZ plant are frequently used to seal environments, prevent subtle invasions, and renew spiritual air. Dead or sick plants, conversely, indicate something is wrong in the energy field. They do not just decorate—they feel, filter, protect.

Moving water, like fountains and aquariums, when well-positioned, attracts prosperity and vital flow.

But if poorly maintained—with dirty, stagnant water or sick fish—it becomes a focus of harmful energies. Water is an element holding memories. And in Feng Shui, it must be honored. A fountain near the entrance, facing into the house, signals energy entering fluidly. Facing outward can mean loss of opportunities.

Sound is also a protective tool. Wind chimes, made of bamboo, metal, or crystal, are placed at strategic points to move Qi and scare away dense energies. They emit frequencies resonating in the subtle field, creating an environment of spiritual vigilance. Each chime's touch is like a call to attention for the invisible, a reminder that there, in that space, consciousness is awake.

In situations where direct spiritual attack is perceived—constant arguments, recurrent illnesses, feelings of oppression—Feng Shui recommends purification rituals including using sea salt in house corners, smudging with herbs like sage and rosemary, and applying protective symbols on windows, like the Chinese character for "peace" written in red, or the heaven trigram itself above the entrance. The color red, incidentally, is one of the most powerful in Feng Shui symbolism. It represents protection, vitality, fire, and action. Using red ribbons to seal doors, snake plants tied with red bows, or even small envelopes called "hongbao," containing intentions, blessings, or consecrated coins, is common. These elements are not superstition. They are symbolic pacts with the energy flow, conscious acts programming the environment to respond positively to human presence.

Feng Shui teaches that protection begins in the visible but acts on the invisible. A cluttered environment, with accumulated objects, debris, or forgotten clothes, becomes fertile ground for Qi stagnation and the action of negative thought-forms. By cleaning, organizing, and beautifying the house consciously, the practitioner performs not just housecleaning—but a light exorcism, a reprogramming of the subtle field.

Protection, according to this tradition, is a constant state of alignment with the natural movement of forces. It is not about building walls, but leaving doors open only to what vibrates harmoniously. It is subtle, daily work requiring sensitivity, presence, humility. The house is not just shelter—it is an extension of the soul. And a protected soul reflects in a protected home.

Practicing protective Feng Shui is, in essence, cultivating everyday spirituality. Grand ceremonies or elaborate rituals are unnecessary if the space is maintained with intention and respect. Every detail—a well-placed plant, an object removed from the path, a window opened in the morning—becomes a sacred gesture. The home ceases to be merely life's backdrop and becomes an active part in the process of spiritual evolution. The house begins to respond, speak silently. And the attentive practitioner perceives: when space aligns, events also reorganize.

This millennial wisdom also teaches that true protection requires balance. An excessively rigid environment, symmetrically impeccable but lifeless, can become energetically arid. Conversely, a home where excess, visual noise, and negligence prevail invites invisible chaos. The path of Feng Shui is the middle way—neither suffocating control nor unconscious abandonment. It is the practice of subtle listening: where Qi wants to flow, where it stopped, what needs more light, what asks for rest. This perception refines over time, with silent observation of the effects each small change provokes on overall harmony.

More than protecting the home against external influences, Feng Shui teaches protecting one's own energy through living with the space. An aligned house is a constant oracle. It reveals when something is off-axis, when it is time to change, when letting go is necessary. And this deep relationship transforms dwelling into an act of consciousness. It is not about "shielding" the home, but making it a place where the spirit can rest, grow, and manifest without noise. Because when the soul is at peace, the surrounding space becomes a shield—and every presence converts into blessing.

Chapter 16
Magic Circles

There are times when the world demands a boundary. Not a wall, not an escape—but a clear line between what may enter and what must remain outside. In ancient times, shamans knew this. Magicians too. Sorcerers, priests, oracles. All of them, at some point in their journeys, understood the need to create a sacred space—a vibrational territory where the laws of the common world hold no sway, where the soul can operate safely, and where the invisible bows to the authority of the awakened spirit. Thus were born magic circles: geometries of power traced between planes, instruments of protection, containment, and evocation.

A magic circle is not just a geometric figure. It is a seal. A silent invocation made with the body, intention, and consciousness. It is a space defined by invisible forces, where light is amplified, shadow is halted, and agreements between worlds are rigorously sealed. Within it, the practitioner is not just protected—they are awake, present, anchored. No force enters without permission. No vibration persists unfiltered.

In the Wiccan tradition, the magic circle is one of the first and most important practices. Before any ritual—be it a simple lunar celebration or a more intense magical operation—the practitioner casts the circle. With the wand, the athame (ceremonial dagger), the hand, or even mental visualization, a space is marked where the four elements are invoked, the cardinal points sealed, and time itself seems suspended. Within the circle, the space becomes a temple. Outside it, the ordinary world remains.

To cast a circle, more than physical instruments are needed. Clarity is required. The practice begins with purifying the environment: energetic sweeping with a ritual broom, smudging with consecrated herbs (sage, rosemary, lavender), and the silence preceding the sacred. Then, the circle is cast clockwise—the direction of creation—while the practitioner invokes the elements: earth to the north, air to the east, fire to the south, water to the west. Each point is marked with a symbol, candle, crystal, or other corresponding object. This creates not just a boundary, but a field of co-creation.

Once cast, the circle is not just a barrier—it is a mirror. Everything placed within it intensifies. A thought becomes form. A desire becomes vibration. A word becomes decree. Therefore, the practitioner must enter the circle with reverence. Common objects, distractions, or disrespect are not brought inside. Every gesture is part of the ritual. Every breath links to the invisible plane. And when the circle is correctly activated, its presence can be felt: the air changes, energy thickens, perception expands.

In ceremonial magic, circles are even more elaborate. Followers of Hermetic or Enochian traditions draw complex circles on the floor with chalk, salt, or consecrated ink, containing Hebrew names of God, astrological symbols, angelic invocations, and planetary seals. These circles are not just protection—they are spiritual machines. They organize reality within a higher logic, allowing the operator to interact with intelligences from other spheres without risk of contamination or attack. Without the circle, the operator is exposed. With the circle, they are in command.

But it wasn't just European magicians who knew the circle's power. In indigenous shamanism, the circle is the basis of almost every ceremony. Drums are played in a circle. Participants sit in a circle. The fire burns in the center. There is no vertical hierarchy—there is circular communion. The circle represents the cycle of life, nature's movement, the dance of planets. It is the space where the spirit manifests safely and clearly. When a circle is cast in an ayahuasca ceremony, for example, it is so the opened portals remain protected. The spirits entering know: that space has been sealed.

Creating a magic circle can also be done without visible instruments. The experienced practitioner can trace it just with the mind, visualizing a line of golden or electric blue light spinning around them, expanding upwards and downwards, forming a vibrational sphere. This type of circle is used in emergency situations— sensing a spiritual attack, entering a hostile environment, sleeping in an unknown place. It is an instant sealing technique. Mind traces. Soul activates. Light forms.

Some circles use crystals for anchoring. Stones like quartz, amethyst, tourmaline, citrine are placed at strategic points around the body or ritual space. Each crystal acts as a vibrational guardian, amplifying intention and sustaining the field. Others use candles, with specific colors according to need: white for spiritual protection, red for strength, blue for peace, black for breaking demands, golden for expanding consciousness. Each element in the circle responds to an archetypal language, and the ensemble creates an energetic symphony that protects, heals, transforms.

It is essential to understand the magic circle should not be broken during the ritual. Leaving it without deactivating is like opening a lab door mid-operation. If necessary to cross the circle, one must "cut a door" with the wand or intention, sealing it upon return. At the work's end, the circle is undone with gratitude. Elements are dismissed. Directions thanked. The line untraced, often counterclockwise, returning space to its natural state. Everything done intentionally. Everything rite.

The circle can also be cast in environments. Before an important meeting, difficult conversation, deep spiritual study, the practitioner can trace an invisible circle around the location, asking for protection, clarity, harmony. One can anoint the four walls with essential oil, draw protection runes with a finger, or leave crystals in the four corners. Thus, the environment becomes temple. Ordinary transmutes into sacred. Any dissonant energy barred at threshold.

It is important to stress the magic circle is not prison. Does not imprison practitioner—liberates. Frees from external noise, mental distractions, energetic interferences. Within it, soul can fly higher. Body relaxes. Mind opens. Spirit operates precisely. That is why so many mystics say: "The true circle is the heart itself." For when heart becomes sacred space, no evil crosses.

In times where boundaries between worlds are increasingly thin, knowing how to cast and maintain a magic circle is essential art. Not just ceremonial resource—spiritual survival tool. Amidst world saturated information, stimuli, dissonant energies, circle is silence. Center. Protection.

When the circle is understood as an extension of one's own being, its practice ceases to be a ritual formality and becomes an expression of awakened consciousness. The tracing is not limited to the moment of the rite but accompanies the practitioner in daily life—each word spoken with intention, each healthy boundary established, each choice aligned with the soul is, in itself, an act of casting a circle. Thus, the entire world can transform into a sacred space, where spiritual discernment reflects in the simplest attitudes, and where the invisible recognizes the seal of one walking in presence.

There is also a silent, profound aspect of the circle rarely mentioned: its capacity to hold. By creating a space where only what is in harmony can enter, the circle becomes a refuge for the most vulnerable parts of the being. In it, forgotten memories can emerge safely, old wounds recognized without fear, subtle visions received without distortion. It is the soul's symbolic womb—a place where what is ready to be born, die, or transform can do so with dignity. Around the fire, under candlelight, or simply enveloped by intention's light, the practitioner finds a deep mirror of themselves. And when the circle finally dissolves, it is not an end, but reintegration. What was activated within continues vibrating, guiding steps, choices in external world. Line once marking limit dissolves, but center remains—alive, pulsating, internalized. Because more than space traced on ground, magic circle is reminder: there is always place where soul is safe. And where soul is safe, everything can begin anew.

Chapter 17
Psychoanalysis of Evil

Not all evil presents with teeth, red eyes, or creeping shadows. Sometimes, evil arrives as a recurring thought, silent sabotage, nameless weight. It settles between memories and silences, walks through the unconscious, finds dwelling in the psyche's open cracks. Spiritual protection, to be complete, cannot ignore this territory. Because where untreated trauma exists, portal exists. Where limiting belief, fissure. And precisely in this hidden space, where soul fragments unnoticed, psychoanalysis finds its place in spiritual defense.

Psychic evil is not metaphorical—it is structured. Carl Gustav Jung, one of 20th century's greatest visionaries, understood this clearly. Knew unconscious not just reservoir repressed desires, but territory inhabited by archetypal forces, living images, potencies which, when poorly integrated, can become destructive. For Jung, collective unconscious houses both gods, demons. Why self-knowledge first bulwark against invisible attack.

Every spiritual obsession begins with unconscious identification. Obsessing spirit connects not by chance—finds attunement. Often, obsessed's own mental field, through unresolved guilts, unintegrated traumas, nurtured resentments, attracts, sustains other's presence. Not guilt—vibrational mechanism. What unseen, grows. What denied, strengthens in dark. Here psychoanalysis becomes protection tool.

Recurring thought, like "I'm not good enough," maintained prolonged time, creates thought-form. This form, once fed emotion—especially fear/anger—gains density. Energetic density is spiritual matter. Can even feed external consciousnesses vibrating same frequency. Not rare people feeding self-destruction thoughts start feeling heavy spiritual presences, attract danger situations. Evil starts not outside. Activated inside.

Emotional repression, taught virtue many cultures, one greatest generators spiritual breaches. What not cried, screams other ways. What unsaid, sickens body. Emotion, unexpressed, converts psychic knot. Accumulated knot becomes vibrational wound. These psychic wounds zones energetic vulnerability. Through them enter obsessors, invasive thoughts, disturbing dreams. Why many contemporary therapeutic systems see unconscious work as spiritual purification tool.

Jung spoke of "shadow"—set personality aspects repressed, forgotten, rejected. Shadow everything person won't admit about self. Paradoxically, more denied, more power gained. Individual claiming always calm, but represses anger, creates aggression shadow possibly exploding uncontrollably or attracting violent situations. What out of consciousness acts behind scenes. Integrating shadow—recognizing, accepting, working with it—act deep spiritual protection.

Spirituality not traversing psyche becomes vulnerable. Individual meditating daily, but not looking emotional wounds, builds illusory peace. Like painting temple cracked walls. Sometime, collapse comes. Why many spiritual practitioners suffer sudden falls, inexplicable crises, unexpected spiritual attacks. Because built fortresses without investigating internal foundations. True spirituality begins where ego ends. Ego ends recognizing wounds need healing.

Limiting beliefs another avenue psychic evil manifests. Phrases like "I don't deserve love," "life is struggle," "world is dangerous" create vibrational fields repelling good, attracting what confirms belief. Mind, in this sense, portal. Used anchor heaven or open house chaos. Who cleans house, but keeps disorganized mind, still vulnerable. True exorcism often starts deep listening session—where silence reveals what speech hides.

Guilt one mental states most exploited by obsessors. Guilt stagnates, sickens, chains. Spirits vibrating suffering frequency feed unresolved human guilts. Why forgiveness—not just others, but self—one most spiritually liberating acts. He who forgives self closes portal. He eternally blaming self keeps doors open assault. Forgiveness, when sincere, seal of light.

Dialogue between psychoanalysis, spirituality not recent. Jung, as cited, deeply studied alchemy, astrology, I Ching, mandalas. Understood symbol unconscious language—through symbol, possible reintegrate soul. Dreams, for him, not mere desire repetitions, but spirit messages. Snake in dream warning, initiation, spiritual presence. Only dreamer deciphers code. This decoding part consciousness shielding process.

Therapeutic hypnosis, well conducted, allows access traumatic memories sustaining obsessive patterns. Many people, after deep regression sessions, report spiritual relief, liberation invisible ties, breaking seemingly unbreakable obsessor bonds. What seen, loses power. Darkness, once illuminated, disappears. Unconscious, once revealed, becomes ally.

Integration psychotherapy, spiritual practices increasingly necessary today's world. Therapist recognizing trauma's energetic dimension guides patient more precisely. Medium understanding pain's psychic mechanisms deals guides, assisted more profoundly. Bridge between worlds needs mature construction. Because no division mind, spirit. Suffering one. Healing also must be.

Many serious spiritual houses now recommend mediums in imbalance seek therapeutic support. Not weakness, but wisdom. Medium emotionally disturbed opens astral field breaches. Leader not knowing own shadow manipulates entire current. Spiritual protection, this level, not just candles, prayers, baths—made truth. Truth, almost always, lives behind fear.

Must say: some obsessors come not outside. Fragmented parts own being. Internal voices fed years, lifetimes, generations. Useless expelling rituals if pattern attracting them lives on. True ritual internal. When look within, say: "I recognize this pain. I care for it now." Then, spirit straightens. Light ignites. Field closes.

Psychoanalysis of evil not about blaming patient. About returning power. Reminding where consciousness, choice. Where choice, path. Unconscious not enemy. Guardian what forgotten. What forgotten, when refound love, becomes part protection.

Journey reintegration, therefore, not denying evil, but conscious listening. Shadow not fought more shadow—fought presence. Presence act sustaining gaze, even facing abyss. Therapeutic work, allied spiritual path, aims not anesthetize pain, but illuminate until reveals origin, message, dormant potency. Some pains, once understood, become masters. Some fears, welcomed, transform courage portals. Some wounds, touched truth, stop bleeding.

Process requires courage. Because requires dismantling personas, questioning inherited beliefs, recognizing still pulsing resentments. Precisely this dive, territory internal ruins, true protection found. Spirit knowing own shadows not frightened others' shadows. Individual recognizing wounds no longer unconsciously opens invasions. More consciousness gained, less space assault remains. Spiritual maturity, above all, lucidity. Lucidity built time, listening, willingness be true oneself.

End, understanding evil psychoanalytic lens understanding every healing path also self-knowledge path. Knowing before protecting external symbols, need clean internal symbols—created pain, still governing silently. Because true shield not iron nor memorized prayers, but consciousness. Where consciousness, light. Where light, evil not sustained.

Chapter 18
Reconnective Healing

Not all healing comes from medicine. Not all illness is physical. There are pains unlocatable in the body, vibrating as distortions in the subtle field, affecting mood, purpose, vitality. They are misalignments of being, ruptures in the invisible mesh sustaining existence's flow. Reconnective healing is born at this point: where the invisible screams, body silences, soul asks remember who it is. More than therapy—return to original frequency. Reconnection with matrix.

So-called reconnective healing is energetic technique surpassing conventional spiritual treatment molds. Acts not just chakras, nor follows fixed protocols. Instead, accesses subtle frequencies beyond etheric mesh, touching directly "cosmic grid"—vibrational network interconnecting all life forms, beyond time, space. Within grid, each being possesses unique pattern, energetic signature which, when distorted, generates imbalance. Reconnective healing aims restore signature, reconnecting individual original frequency.

Many call technique "quantum healing," but goes beyond science/conventional spirituality nomenclatures.

Depends not patient belief, nor requires years preparation. When practiced someone attuned these frequencies, simply happens. As if person tunes internal radio station transmitting regenerative, organizing, clean vibration. Vibration corrects not just physical body, but emotional, mental, spiritual bodies too.

Manifestations during reconnective healing session intense. Many report sensations heat, cold, tingling, pulsations, vivid mental images, sudden emotions, spontaneous crying, even visions light beings. Not spectacle. Realignment. Body, soul recognize vibration familiar. Something forgotten suddenly recalled. Remembrance brings healing.

This type energy work widely disseminated names like Eric Pearl, but roots older, dispersed shamanic traditions, hermetic practices, planetary wisdoms channeled sensitives worldwide. Concept body possesses "light field" restructurable specific frequencies not new. Egyptians, Vedic seers, Tao masters already knew intuitively these truths.

Cosmic grid—also called universal mesh—interconnected network energy, consciousness linking each being whole. Within grid, no separation healer, healed, mind, matter, here, there. Therapist acting reconnective healing sends not energy—accesses grid, allows flow through self. Healer's role channel, silent bridge between consciousness dimensions.

Unlike many energetic practices involving laying hands, visualization, directed intention, reconnective healing requires practitioner "get out way." Commands not process. Just tunes. Cosmic mesh intelligence does rest. Intelligence knows being needs more than conscious ego. Often, session result not what patient wanted—what soul needed. Sometimes includes intense purging processes, emotional detox, path reconfiguration.

Spiritual protection offered practice not external barrier—internal restructuring. When being's frequency elevated original vibration, naturally repels what not resonates. Dense entities, negative thought-forms, destructive emotional patterns simply find no more space. Frequency becomes incompatible evil. Like orchestra tuning instruments: harmony expels noise.

Practically, reconnective healing performed presence or distance. Cosmic mesh recognizes no geographic limits. Acts through intention, vibrational connection. Many therapists report sessions via video call, even patient sleeping, effects intense as presence. Because this field, time relative. Space malleable. Spirit sovereign.

Before session, ideal patient receptive, state surrender. Not necessary believe, essential not resist. Resistance closes channels. Surrender opens. Environment quiet, clean, protected. Some use crystals, candles, incense facilitate anchoring, but reconnective healing essence beyond elements. Pure field.

During session, therapist positions around body, not touching. Feels hands, subtle perception field. Light movements, almost imperceptible, indicate where frequency manifesting most intensely. Sometimes hand drawn specific point—joint, organ, chakra—remains until field reorganizes. Other times, flow passes entire body like invisible light river.

Post-session period great importance. Many report lucid dreams, powerful insights, synchronicities, spontaneous healings, sometimes emotional crises preceding relief. Field cleaning. Body processing. Soul reorganizing layers. Therefore, after reconnective healing session, recommend rest, hydration, light food, introspection. Post-healing silence part remedy.

Some ask: this healing definitive? Answer: profound. But free will remains. Field reconfigured, but if individual returns same mental, emotional, behavioral patterns generating imbalance, misalignment can return. Therefore, reconnective healing also call transformation. Cleanses, but requires maintenance. Heals, but invites continuous consciousness.

Science, still timid before practices, begins approaching. Studies biophotonics, toroidal fields, cardiac coherence, neuroplasticity opening doors new understanding health, spirituality. Independent researchers documented changes brain electrical pattern, heart electromagnetic field during reconnective healing sessions. But more than measuring, need feel. Because healing not just measurable—experiential.

Reconnective healing replaces not conventional medical treatments. Complements. Often, transcends. Acts where medicine not reaches. Treats invisible. Invisible, once treated, transforms visible. Body responds what soul vibrates. Reconnected soul vibrates health.

Greatest secret practice simple: healing comes not outside. Emerges within, when field restored, remembrance unity returns. Therapist just holds mirror. Being, seeing self whole again, begins healing self.

Reconnective healing's true potency lies subtlety. No formulas, salvation promises—frequency. Frequency not argued, felt. Why seeks not convince, just touch. Interacting this field, being not just heals: remembers. Remembers what was before pain, fear, time distortions. Remembrance organizes chaos. What seemed noise reveals rhythm. What sounded loss transforms restart. Accessing original frequency, individual refinds truth. No greater healing than inhabiting truth fully.

This energetic approach also forces review what understand health. Maybe healthy not just symptomless, but coherent. Coherent mind, body, soul, field. Coherent what desired, thought, done. When integrity begins restoring, entire being vibrates different note. World, responding vibration like intelligent mirror, reorganizes around new pattern. Why often, after deep healing, not just pain disappears—relationships transform, paths open, destiny changes route.

This type healing, therefore, not endpoint. Return point. Reminder we vaster what feel, think, suffer. Always available, silent, luminous field recognizing us whole, even when feel broken. Touching field, something rearranges—not effort, but resonance. Reconnecting larger mesh, become again music within universe orchestra.

Chapter 19
Light Codes

There is language type not written letters, nor spoken mouth. Pulses numbers, vibrates forms, reveals secrets only those learned see soul eyes. They are light codes—numeric combinations, sacred geometries not just symbolizing divine, but activating body, mind, energy field. When used consciously, codes become living spiritual protection instruments, acting keys locking dimensional doors, sealing being against invisible invasions.

Not superstition. Nor common numerology. Light codes belong vibrational lineage transcending religions, doctrines. Operate reality levels where symbol, sound more real matter. Each number possesses force field. Each geometric form carries order pattern. When forces activated clear intention, modulate energy field like symphonies adjusting silent environment. Protection, this case, comes not outside—emerges alignment higher frequencies.

Best known numeric codes—like 111, 222, 333, 777, 999—just surface deep vibrational ocean. 111, for example, considered immediate manifestation portal: seeing repeatedly, many report synchronicity experiences, intensified intuitions, "spiritual vigilance" sensation. 777 regarded divine protection code, signature guides', masters' presence signaling path aligned. But number repetition not coincidence—resonance. Individual's vibrational field attracts number needs decoding.

Decoding, however, not just logical mind. Requires vibrational attunement. Number must be felt, chanted, visualized. Become part field. Why many practitioners use light codes writing papers, placing under pillows, tattooing discreetly body energy points, tracing fingertips skin/chest, where heart chakra resides. Others chant mantras—"one-one-one," "seven-seven-seven"—each repetition invoking corresponding frequency.

Besides numbers, light codes also manifest geometric forms known sacred geometry. Flower Life one most potent examples. Composed multiple perfectly overlapped circumferences, represents creation matrix—vibrational structure everything existing. Meditating Flower Life, tracing paper, positioning under food/water, using amulet/altar, way bring vibrational order chaos. Charged spaces, form acts neutralizing distorted fields.

Other symbols include Seed Life, Metatron's Cube, Tetrahedron, Dodecahedron, Fire Triangle, among many others. Each operates specific frequency range, aligning being higher forces. Metatron's Cube, for example, known ability cleanse environments dense entities, restore energetic order, create almost impenetrable protection mesh around physical, astral body. When visualized rotating, as if spinning self, reorganizes field.

There are also channeled codes, received mediums, sensitives worldwide. One best known Grabovoi system, developed Russian Grigori Grabovoi. Proposes specific numeric sequences different intentions: health, protection, prosperity, emotional balance. Example, sequence 520 741 regarded code immediate problem solution. 9187948181 supposedly energetic protection sequence. But sequences' power not just numbers—intention activated with.

Activating light code act presence. Practitioner enter meditative state, breathe consciously, visualize number/form, chant/repeat mentally absolute focus. Vibration generated union mind, sound, form penetrates energy field layers, adjusting dissonant frequencies, sealing field against external influences. Done regularly, process strengthens aura, makes thoughts clearer, drastically reduces susceptibility spiritual attacks.

Codes also used protect environments. Paper numeric sequence placed behind door, sticker sacred geometry wall, even visualizing symbol floating room four corners, ways seal space. Many report immediate environment changes: conflicts cease, energy calms, hostile visitors withdraw. Because where vibration high, dense not remains.

But how recognize which code use? Answer not books—personal attunement. Code appearing repeatedly individual life, emerging dreams, causing shiver/recognition sensation, generally what field most needs. Intuition soul language. This path, best guide.

Light codes also used rituals. During purification bath, chant code 333 visualizing water filling white light; sleeping, repeat mentally 888 while visualizing golden shield enveloping body; waking, trace finger air sequence 741 mental alignment. Simple practices, profound energetic repercussion. Not complexity activates sacred—consciousness.

Some combine light codes other protection tools: crystals, mantras, prayers, religious symbols. Integration possible, often amplifies results. Clear quartz energized sequence 777, positioned home center, acts continuous protection beacon. Necklace Flower Life, consecrated number 1111, becomes vibrational anchor. Secret lies coherence intention, symbol, action.

Need, however, responsibility. Light codes use not curiosity, distraction, quick consumption spirit. Living frequencies, conscious, demand respect. Activated without clarity, cause physical discomforts, intense dreams, emotional purges. Because every deep cleanse starts exposing what hidden. Light, entering, illuminates everything—including what avoided seeing.

Those dedicating study, practice codes know journey continuous. Each new number, form, reality layer reveals. Perception sharpens. Intuition refines. Body more sensitive. Soul, more protected. Because true protection not shielding—attunement what above noise. Being frequency pure, true, eternal.

This light language, fully integrated, transforms how individual moves world. No longer just using code need moments, but becoming it. Body becomes living mandala, gaze recognizes subtle patterns where before just chance, daily life read sacred text written symbols. Practice ceases being eventual, becomes state—way being presence, listening invisible, dialoguing universe through own signs.

Deeply liberating understanding protection comes not force, but harmony. Not necessary erect walls when emit light. Light codes, this sense, vibrational reminders true security lies living resonance whole. When field attuned cosmic order, chaos noises find nowhere anchor. Being becomes well-tuned instrument: any dissonance stands out, quickly adjusted. Soul, anchored original frequency, becomes unattainable lower vibrations.

Finally, more than protection system, light codes paths remembrance. Add not something being—just reveal what always there, under forgetfulness layers. Each number, form, sequence note silent chant soul returning home. This return, everything reorganizes. Light imposes not—reveals. Once revealed, awakened being never returns previous unconsciousness. Carries key itself. Is code itself.

Chapter 20
Comparative Exorcisms

There exists point where invisible becomes unsustainable. Where other's presence—not physical other, but other vibrating dissonance—begins imposing consciousness, body, senses. This presence, many traditions named possession. Practice expelling it, exorcism. But exorcism, spiritual concept, transcends theatrical scenes popularized films. Essentially, act vibrational realignment, soul return center, being reintegration light.

Exorcism, ritual practice, exists practically all planet spiritual traditions. Because evil presence—understood here consciousness deviation, obsession, spiritual invasion—constant humanity history. Each culture, own way, developed techniques, prayers, seals, formulas restore spiritual balance when breaks. What changes names, symbols, myths—essence always same: liberate.

Christianity, especially Roman Catholicism, exorcism formal ritual, recognized Church legitimate, structured practice. Rituale Romanum, text organizing Catholic rites since 1614, contains specific instructions Exorcismus in Satanam et Angelos Apostaticos—Greater Exorcism. Ritual requires exorcist priest episcopal authorization, rigorous spiritual preparation, obedience precise liturgical sequence. Psalms, biblical passages, Trinity invocations recited Latin, possessed's name never confused entity manifesting. During rite, exorcist demands, Christ's name, spirit abandon possessed body. Use sacred objects—crucifixes, holy water, relics, candles—common, focus spiritual authority exorcist. Fights not own strength, but faith, doctrine, celestial hierarchy strength. Many reports describe sudden voice changes, aversion sacred symbols, hidden knowledge, disproportionate strength during possession episodes. True exorcism seeks not spectacle—seeks liberation.

Protestantism, especially Pentecostal, Neo-Pentecostal branches, exorcism takes different forms. Often known "deliverance session," type spiritual intervention more direct, less ritualistic, deeply based Jesus name authority. Pastor/worker cries out, prays aloud, lays hands, confronts entity Christ's name, demands withdrawal. Spiritual combat lived personal battle God's servant, oppressing spirit. Chants, fasts, prayer pillars sustaining practitioner's force field.

Afro-Brazilian religions, like Umbanda, Candomblé, exorcism understood not "expulsion," but "cleansing"/"descarrego." Possession itself not seen negative—contrary, incorporation essential religious practice. What fought not spiritual presence itself, but presence imposing without permission, sucking, enslaving, oppressing. These cases, medium prepared channel oppressing entity, assisted house guides, who dismantle, instruct, remove it. Smudging specific herbs, chanted points, cleansing baths, use pemba (ritual chalk), consecrated drinks common liberation rites.

Kardecist Spiritism, process more subtle, therapeutic. Spiritual obsession understood karmic link obsessor, obsessed. Doutrinador (instructor), mediumistic sessions, dialogues disturbing spirit, offering enlightenment, forgiveness, redirection. Focus not expelling, but evangelizing. Spirit treated not enemy, but sick sibling. Model, based Allan Kardec teachings, seeks healing both sides—incarnate, discarnate.

Islam, exorcism known ruqya—set practices based Quran recitation, Allah names invocation. Surahs like Al-Fatiha, Al-Baqara, Al-Ikhlas repeated purification, spell breaking intention. Recited water used drink, wash body, sprinkle environments. Ruqya practiced Quran scholars, respected piety, knowledge. Djinns—spiritual beings cited Quran—frequently associated possessions. Ruqya seeks dissolve link human being, these entities, restoring spiritual peace.

Tibetan Buddhism, possession seen result karmic imbalances, spiritual vulnerabilities. Exorcism, called chod some schools, involves complex rituals practitioner offers own symbolic body banquet afflicted spirits. Goal not expel, but feed, calm, release. Other rites involve mandala creation, specific mantra recitation, use sacred instruments like damaru (drum), dorje (scepter), plus convocation protective deities like Mahakala, Vajrapani, Palden Lhamo. Trained lama/monk acts channel between worlds, undoing vibrational ties causing suffering.

Despite cultural differences, all exorcism rites share common point: invocation higher spiritual authority. Be God, Jesus, Olorum, Allah, Buddha, Higher Self, always through transcendent force liberation happens. Exorcist, however experienced, acts not alone. Connects, anchors, aligns. Connection holds power.

But exorcism not risk-free ritual. Unprepared, vain, emotionally unstable practitioner hit entity field. Absorb pain fragments, suffer later spiritual attacks, lose process control. Why all traditions demand purity, preparation, vigilance, humility. True exorcist not who shouts loudest—who remains internally silent amidst chaos.

Modern times, spiritual possession often confused psychological disorders, discernment fundamental. Not every disturbance obsession. Not every internal voice entity. Responsible exorcism requires listening, analysis, prudence. Alliance spirituality, science fundamental avoid abuses, misdiagnoses. Poorly conducted ritual cause irreversible mind, body damage. Exorcism last resort—not first.

But when necessary, liberating. Breaks bond. Illuminates darkness. Returns being center. Being, once remade, recognizes: what dominated merely reflection what forgotten illuminate.

Amidst diversity methods, rituals, what truly defines exorcism effectiveness not form, but intention anchored inner truth. Each culture finds own spiritual imaginary instruments making sense within worldview. All cases, authentic liberation only happens profound recognition human being not just victim external forces, also creator—conscious/unconscious—bonds keeping trapped. Exorcism then becomes less combat, more revelation: power resides soul clarity.

Also silent element permeating all rites, rarely named: compassion. When exorcism performed brutally, without listening/empathy, might remove entity, hardly promotes healing. When space understand manifesting spirit pain, something deeper moves. Evil, named, welcomed origin, often loses strength. Mature exorcist imposes not light—sustains light until dissolves darkness. This sustenance, often silent, transforms rite miracle.

End, exorcise remember. Remind lost spirit can return. Remind possessed has power. Remind exorcist just channel. When remembrance happens, liberation inevitable—not force, but clarity. Because nothing recognized light manages remain rooted shadow. Why more than battle good, evil, exorcism reunion parts forgotten way back.

Chapter 21
Crystals and Earth Mines

Among the silent layers of the Earth, there are sleeping guardians. They do not scream, nor move, but they vibrate. They are ancient, witnesses to the planet's formation, charged with memories, codes, frequencies that cannot be heard by common ears. They are the crystals—pure portions of mineral consciousness, condensed into form, color, and brilliance. They are not inanimate objects. They are living allies, capable of sustaining fields, purifying environments, aligning chakras, and protecting against invisible forces operating at the edge of everyday perception.

The use of crystals as spiritual tools dates back to ancient civilizations. The Egyptians lined their sarcophagi with lapis lazuli. The Mayans used quartz for solar rituals. The Hindus described stones as manifestations of devas—elemental intelligences linked to matter. And shamans from different continents knew: within the earth's veins hide minerals that not only heal but protect. For each crystal is a seal. A fragment of nature's hidden language.

Clear quartz, considered the most versatile of all crystals, is the stone of amplification. It doesn't just emit one frequency but resonates with everything entrusted to it. When programmed with a clear intention—be it for protection, healing, or spiritual expansion—it acts as a continuous emitter of that frequency. Placed under the pillow, under the bed, or worn around the neck, it gently expands the personal field and repels dissonant energies. But its strength depends on the clarity of the programmer. For clear quartz is like a mirror: it reflects what is within.

Black tourmaline, on the other hand, is a guardian of boundaries. A dense, dark stone, deeply linked to the earth element, it does not soften—it blocks. Its presence is sentinel. Where there is black tourmaline, there is field delineation. Used around the environment, at the four corners of a room or space, it creates an invisible seal preventing the entry of opportunistic entities, astral larvae, dense thought-forms. When worn as a pendant or carried in a pocket, it protects against psychic attacks, envy, the evil eye, and even electromagnetic radiation.

Obsidian, meanwhile, is a crystal of revelation. Born from volcanic fire, it carries the power to bring to the surface what was hidden. Its energy is not comfortable. It does not welcome—it shows. Therefore, it is used cautiously in processes of deep self-knowledge. When placed in the field, it activates unconscious memories, denied truths, forgotten traumas. But at the same time, it creates a kind of energetic cocoon preventing these truths from turning into spiritual breaches. In protection rituals, obsidian is used to identify the origin of subtle attacks and to seal the field after intense cleansings.

These are just three examples among dozens of crystals acting as agents of vibrational defense. Amethyst, linked to the crown chakra, protects against mental and spiritual intoxication. Sodalite, acting on the throat chakra, prevents psychic manipulations and spiritual lies. Citrine, associated with the solar plexus, dissipates emotional attacks and restores self-esteem. Each stone vibrates at a specific frequency, and this frequency, when aligned with the practitioner's need, transforms into a shield.

But crystals do not work alone. They need programming. This means their energy must be awakened, aligned, and directed. Programming can be done by laying on of hands, conscious breathing, verbalized intention, or meditation. The practitioner holds the crystal, silences the mind, connects with the Earth, and transmits their intention clearly. The stone registers. And from then on, it continuously emits this intention.

This process must be followed by periodic energetic cleansing, as crystals absorb the frequencies they contact. A tourmaline placed in a charged environment, for example, acts as a filter—but filtering saturates it. And if not cleansed, it begins to reverberate what it absorbed. The most common forms of cleansing include immersion in water with coarse salt, exposure to sunlight or moonlight, smudging with herbs like sage, rue, or rosemary, and using sounds—like bells, Tibetan bowls, or specific mantras.

Besides cleansing, there is energetic charging. A clean crystal can be energized with sunlight (for stones linked to fire and action), moonlight (for crystals of intuition and psychic protection), or by the practitioner's own intention. Some also use the technique of placing them on amethyst geodes or in contact with other larger crystals. The important thing is that the crystal is not just clean—it needs nourishment.

Positioning crystals on the body during meditation or protection practices also requires attention. In situations of spiritual attack, for example, it is recommended to place a black tourmaline between the feet, an obsidian on the navel, and an amethyst at the center of the forehead. This combination creates a defense axis preventing invasions and realigning the energy field. In environments, it is common to form mandalas with crystals, using specific stones to create geometric designs that seal the space and elevate its vibration.

There are also myths about "bloodthirsty" or high-risk crystals. Some practitioners report that certain crystals, when used unprepared, trigger difficult processes: intense dreams, emotional purges, physical symptoms. This does not mean the stone is negative—but that it acted profoundly, activating latent patterns. Therefore, crystals like obsidian, moldavite, and hematite should be used responsibly and accompanied by grounding practices.

Science is beginning to touch these mysteries at the edges. The phenomenon of piezoelectricity, for example, shows that certain crystals, like quartz, generate electric currents when pressed. This property is used in watches, computers, and precision instruments.

But what few mention is that this same principle also operates in the subtle fields of the human body. By keeping a crystal close to the body—especially during intense emotion—an interaction field is activated between the stone and the energy centers. The spiritual technology of crystals, therefore, is not superstition: it is merely science yet unnamed.

In traditions like Wicca, shamanism, and Afro-Brazilian religions, crystals are consecrated with songs, dances, prayers, and offerings. They are treated as living beings, honored as allies. Some say each crystal has a name, a personality, a history. And that when ignored, it loses its shine. When respected, it vibrates. This relationship between practitioner and crystal defines its potency. It is not the stone's size, nor its monetary value—it is the spiritual bond.

In the end, understanding crystals as earth mines means recognizing the Earth as a living organism. And that its depths produce not only metals or coal, but crystalline consciousnesses ready to assist in humanity's protection, healing, and spiritual expansion. He who walks with crystals walks with fragments of the planet's soul. And this soul, when awakened, protects with the firmness of one who has never forgotten its purpose.

There is also a less explored, yet profoundly transformative aspect: listening to crystals. When the practitioner sits in absolute silence and full presence before a stone, something subtle reveals itself. Not words, but impressions. Not ideas, but pulsations. It is as if each crystal has its own song, a vibration translating ancestral knowledge, impossible to capture by rational means. By opening to this listening, humans recognize there are wisdoms not coming from above, but from within the Earth. These are teachings that do not shout, merely resonate. And it is in this listening that many receive intuitions, images, and even spiritual guidance orienting the path with unexpected clarity.

This kind of bond, however, requires commitment. It is not enough to acquire a crystal and expect it to resolve what has not yet been faced within. Crystals do not do the work for anyone—they are amplifiers, yes, but also demanding mirrors and masters. They ask for presence, truth, purpose. Working with crystals is also being shaped by them. It is allowing one's own density to be polished by the vibrations of other forms of consciousness. And the more honest this process, the more crystals respond. Some say they shine brighter. Others, that they warm in the hands. Still others, that they speak. Each experience is unique, but all point to the same center: the living relationship between human and mineral.

For all these reasons, dealing with crystals involves not just practices or techniques, but a reunion. A return to something very ancient, pulsing beneath our feet since before language and history. Crystals are not accessories to spirituality—they are portals. And by recognizing them as such, we enter a silent alliance with the Earth itself, which, through them, continues to teach, protect, and remind us that we are part of a much larger whole, where every stone, every pulse, every sparkle has a role to fulfill.

Chapter 22
Ayahuasca and Purging

In the heart of the forest, where civilization loses its voice and nature whispers in forgotten frequencies, exists a secret walking between the world of the living and the realm of spirits. It is not a plant, nor just a brew. It is a portal. A plant spirit that, when invoked correctly, takes the being to the depths of themselves, where the roots of evil, pain, illness reside. This secret has a name: Ayahuasca. And its medicine is not light. It tears, spins, purges. Because true protection begins with cleansing what was denied.

Ayahuasca, a sacred brew of Amazonian origin, results from uniting two master plants: the Banisteriopsis caapi vine and the leaves of Psychotria viridis, or chacruna. One provides MAO inhibitors (harmaline, harmine), the other contains DMT, a psychedelic substance naturally present in the human body and various plants. Alone, these substances do not cause the characteristic hallucinogenic effect. Together, they create a bridge between worlds, activating the pineal gland, expanding consciousness, and temporarily dissolving the veil between dimensions.

But it is not the effect that defines ayahuasca—it is the intention with which it is ingested. In the correct context, under the guidance of masters, shamans, or experienced facilitators, the brew becomes an instrument of deep purification. The purge, a term used to describe the process of vomiting, diarrhea, intense sweating, or convulsive crying during the experience, is not a side effect. It is the cleansing ritual itself. It is the body, spirit, and mind releasing dense energies, adhered entities, crystallized traumas. It is the organic exorcism of trapped emotions.

In indigenous traditions like those of the Huni Kuin, Yawanawá, Ashaninka, and others, ayahuasca—also called nixi pae, daime, or yagé—is considered a conscious being. A spirit that teaches, guides, demands, and heals. By ingesting the brew, the practitioner is not consuming a drug, but making a pact. An agreement with forest forces for their soul to be reviewed, reoriented, liberated. Therefore, preparation before the ritual is crucial: light diet, sexual abstinence, inner silence, fasting. The body must be clean for the spirit to enter.

The spiritual protection provided by ayahuasca is not immediate—it is procedural. During the ritual, the practitioner's energy field expands, making them more sensitive and, paradoxically, more vulnerable. Thus, rituals are always conducted in a circle, with sacred songs (icaros or hymns), constant smudging, and often, the presence of guardians trained to handle intense spiritual manifestations. It is not uncommon for entities to manifest during the work. They come because they were called, consciously or not, by the participant's vibrational field. And there, in the brew's strength, they are confronted, liberated, instructed.

The purge is not only physical. It is emotional and spiritual. Some people relive old traumas, cry for forgotten pains, face memories of other lives, see symbolic forms of their fears, desires, addictions. Others dive into cosmic landscapes, see living geometries, speak with their guides, receive direct instructions from the plant. Some see snakes, jaguars, birds, beings of light. Some just listen. Each experience is unique. And all are real, even if symbolic.

That is why using ayahuasca requires respect and discernment. Outside the ritualistic context, without preparation, without accompaniment, the brew can open dangerous portals. It amplifies what is within. If there is chaos, it will be exposed. If there is fear, it will take form. Therefore, many facilitators refuse to offer the brew to people in unstable emotional states or under the effect of psychiatric medications. The risk is not in the plant—it is in what it reveals.

Alongside ayahuasca, in many rituals, other sacred medicines are used. Rapé, for example—a fine powder made from tobacco and specific herbs—is blown into the nostrils to cleanse energy channels and focus protection. Its action is quick, intense, centering. It also acts as a sealer after the purge, reorganizing the practitioner's vibrational field. Sananga eye drops are sometimes used to sharpen vision, both physical and spiritual. Santo Daime, in some branches, blends Christian hymns with the brew's use, creating a bridge between indigenous cosmology and Western tradition symbolism.

Modern science is beginning to recognize ayahuasca's therapeutic effects. Research indicates it can help treat depression, anxiety, addictions, post-traumatic stress disorders. But these studies are still superficial compared to the experience's complexity. The true healing provided by the plant is not just psychological. It is energetic. And often, spiritual.

During the ritual, ayahuasca not only reveals—it acts. Many people report feeling invisible hands working on their bodies, as if operated on by spiritual doctors. Others see threads being cut, ropes untied, shadows dissolved. Some scream, dance, remain in absolute silence. Everything is expression. Everything is purgation. And each reaction is the body's language trying to translate the moving invisible.

The spiritual protection provided by ayahuasca manifests after the purge. When the field is cleansed, the body remade, the mind clearer, the spirit more whole, life changes. Addictions disappear. Nightmares cease. Relationships reorganize. Paths open. Because the soul, now unobstructed, returns to emitting its original frequency. And this frequency, in itself, is already a shield.

But the work does not end with the ritual. What the plant shows needs integration. That is why there is so much talk about the "post-ayahuasca process." Meditation, writing, therapy, silence. The plant shows—but the human must transform. Without this integration, the experience becomes just a delusion. With it, it becomes medicine.

It is important to remember that ayahuasca is not for everyone. Some have different paths. Some are not ready. And that is okay. The forest calls those prepared to listen. And when it calls, it is not about escape, nor seeking ecstasy. It is about surrender. The plant does not heal capriciously. It heals when the soul says yes.

In the end, understanding ayahuasca as a tool for spiritual protection means recognizing that the greatest defense against evil is truth. And that this truth, when experienced in an expanded state of consciousness, dissolves darkness more effectively than any mantra or talisman. Because the light it ignites is the one that already existed—merely covered by layers of pain.

This unveiling process promoted by ayahuasca is, above all, an invitation to humility. The brew offers no guarantees of comfort nor promises of constant ecstasy—on the contrary, it often guides the practitioner through inner corridors locked long ago. In these crossings, the individual confronts their own mental and emotional constructions, naked before the truth of what they have become and what they need to let go of. It is here that the purge reveals its true power: not as an act of suffering, but as the moment when what was silenced finally finds passage. Crying, screaming, trembling, or remaining motionless are just physical expressions of something much deeper—the soul cleaning its house.

That is why those returning from a serious ayahuasca ritual often carry a specific kind of silence in their eyes. Not the silence of ignorance, but of reverence. Something was touched. Something was moved. And this something, being moved, also changes the view of the world. Toxic relationships lose strength. Empty ambitions dissolve. Sensitivity sharpens. Many feel a stronger connection with nature, start paying more attention to their dreams, and develop an intuition that previously seemed dormant. This is because, by cleansing the field, ayahuasca not only expels what harms—it restores what is essential. And in this restoration, spiritual protection becomes a natural state, not a fabricated defense.

The spirit of ayahuasca protects not with walls, but with lucidity. And it is this lucidity that guides the practitioner's path after the ritual. More than a shield, it offers a new vision: that true spiritual security comes not from hiding, but from revealing oneself. From aligning with what is true. The plant shows, cleanses, guides—but who protects, in the end, is the being itself, reminded of its original strength. Because when the soul vibrates again at its full frequency, no shadow remains for long. The light born from encountering truth is, in itself, the most powerful of protections.

Chapter 23
Guardian Angels

Since the beginning of time, there have been records of beings of light walking alongside humans, invisible, attentive, silent. They do not impose, nor interfere directly, but watch, guide, protect. They are messengers between worlds, bridges between the divine and human, shadows of light hovering in decisive moments, sighs of pain, whispers of prayer. They are the guardian angels. And their presence is constant, even if unnoticed.

Belief in guardian angels transcends religions. It is present in Christianity, Islam, Spiritism, esoteric traditions, and even certain branches of mystical Judaism. They are described as spiritual intelligences designated by a higher order to accompany each human being during their earthly journey. This is not metaphor or allegory—it is a subtle reality, recognized by thousands of reports and deep spiritual experiences.

In Christianity, the figure of the guardian angel is clear. The Catechism of the Catholic Church states that "from infancy to death human life is surrounded by their watchful care and intercession." They are unique beings, not repeated, remaining with the individual from birth until return to the spiritual plane. Their role is not to prevent suffering, but to ensure the soul's life plan is not diverted by external or internal forces beyond its control. The guardian angel does not protect the body—protects the purpose.

The guardian angel prayer, taught to children as a simple resource of faith, is actually a formula for activating presence. By reciting it with intention and awareness, a vibrational link is created between the conscious mind and the angel's field. The text, simple in structure, functions as a key: "Angel of God, my guardian dear, to whom God's love commits me here, ever this day be at my side, to light and guard, to rule and guide. Amen." This prayer, repeated softly at dawn or before sleep, seals the spiritual field, prevents subtle intrusions, and strengthens intuition.

In Islam, angels are called malaikah, created directly from light. Among them, two accompany each person: Raqib and Atid, recording good and bad deeds, but there is also a tradition recognizing the existence of a personal protection angel, a vigilant spirit designated by Allah to watch over each faithful. The Quran, in several passages, mentions angels as guardians of good, messengers between God and humans, purely obedient, without ego. Their role is to act according to divine order—flawlessly, without deviation.

In Kardecist Spiritism, guardian angels are understood as elevated spirits, often spiritual guides of higher hierarchy, who undertake the commitment to accompany a certain soul in its incarnation. These spirits do not impose their presence—they respect free will. When ignored, they merely observe. But when called sincerely, they act forcefully. Allan Kardec's psychography reveals that many of these spirits have already passed through multiple incarnations and reached such a degree of purification that they no longer need to reincarnate. Their mission now is to serve.

In mediumistic experiences, it is common for the guardian angel to manifest as a subtle presence: a hand on the shoulder during tears, a light in the midst of darkness, a silent voice saying "don't go" when the abyss approaches. These signs should not be underestimated. They are how the invisible communicates with the sensitive. And he who learns to listen to the angel also learns to avoid unnecessary pain.

The spiritual protection offered by the guardian angel is refined. It does not prevent challenges, but softens falls. It does not eliminate wrong choices, but opens doors for return. It is a compass, not a shield. When a person aligns with their angel, paths become clearer, coincidences more frequent, answers quicker. This is because the angel acts by reorganizing life's invisible threads, influencing encounters, untying knots, bringing opportunities that sustain the soul's plan.

There are specific forms of invocation strengthening this bond. Lighting a white candle in a clean, quiet environment, writing a letter to the angel, calling them by name—even if unknown—and meditating with the intention of hearing them. There are also ancient practices consisting of asking the guardian angel for a sign before sleeping, and upon waking, observing the first thought, sound, or image. Angels communicate through synchronicities, universe whispers, symbols—never imposition.

In esoteric traditions like Kabbalah, there is an angelic hierarchy composed of 72 names, known as the angels of the Shem HaMephorash. Each of these angels rules a specific degree of the zodiac wheel and is associated with a day of the year, specific energy, spiritual function. By knowing their Kabbalistic angel—calculable based on birth date—the individual can establish a more intimate relationship with their protective frequency. Sacred codes, like Hebrew names, are used as invocation seals. And these seals, when drawn or visualized, create fields of light around the practitioner.

But an important warning: not every being of light is, in fact, light. There are entities disguising themselves as angels, mimicking frequencies, approaching with gentle appearance, but whose vibration carries distortion. The key to discernment lies in the felt vibration. The true guardian angel never generates fear, never forces, never demands. Their presence is peace. Is love. Is silent certainty. Therefore, when contacting any entity, it is essential to ask clearly: "In the name of true light, do you come?" And feel the answer in the body, field, heart.

For those working with mediumship, contact with the guardian angel is a balancing factor. They are the true field coordinator, responsible for maintaining the medium's axis, preventing external forces from overriding the mission. In deeper rituals, the angel may manifest as an authority figure—not to conduct the work, but to ensure it remains aligned with the greater plan. Therefore, many experienced mediums invoke their angels before any session: light candles, pray, seal the space with the light they bring.

Is it possible for the guardian angel to depart? No. But it is possible for their voice to become inaudible. The world's noise, addictions, inflated ego, pride, fear—all act as vibrational barriers. The angel remains present, but the connection weakens. And a weak connection results in disorientation. Rekindling this bond requires humility. A prayer whispered at night. A sincere request for help. A tear admitting: "I forgot you." And the angel, faithful as only beings of light know how to be, responds.

In the end, understanding the guardian angel's role in spiritual protection means understanding that the universe never abandons us. That there has always been a loving presence beside us, waiting for us to look at it. Remember it. Call it. Because evil, however aggressive, cannot resist the frequency of a heart aligned with its guardian.

This bond with the guardian angel also redefines how we relate to the idea of protection itself. Instead of seeking external, reactive defense often based on fear, the angel's presence teaches building an internal fortress, made of lucidity, faith, and sensitive listening. This protection is not expressed in miraculous spectacles, but in small shifts of daily life: a delay avoiding an accident, an intuition preventing a harmful choice, a dream guiding a path. These are subtle details that, when recognized, reveal an intelligent, loving pattern sustaining the journey—a pattern only revealed to those accepting walking in partnership with the invisible.

There is also a profoundly transformative aspect in this contact: the remembrance that we were never alone. Even in the darkest moments, even on days when faith seemed absent, the angel was there. Silent, patient, respectful. This constant loving presence—which does not abandon, demand, only remains—serves as a mirror for our own potential for unconditional love. Realizing this opens something in our field: a kind of trust independent of proof, courage born from deep knowing that, whatever happens, a presence watches over us, knows our essence, and acts, always, in the name of the greater good.

Therefore, cultivating this relationship is not just an act of devotion—it is a choice of spiritual lucidity. It is deciding to live attuned to a guide knowing hidden paths, understanding the soul's timing, knowing when to intervene and when to just observe. The guardian angel is not just a protector—is a mission companion, a silent ally reminding us daily that we are loved and guided. And when this certainty settles in the heart, life changes. Because he who walks in alliance with light no longer fears shadows.

Chapter 24
Defensive Psychography

There exists a writing not born from the rational mind. It flows from another source, traverses time, ignores grammar, escapes control. It pulses from beyond, touches paper like a silent wind, leaving traces of the invisible in lines carrying messages, warnings, guidance. This writing belongs neither to ego nor author. It is psychography. And when practiced consciously, becomes one of the most refined tools of spiritual protection.

Psychography, according to Spiritist and esoteric tradition, is the ability to write under the direct influence of spiritual entities. It is not just inspiration—it is incorporation of the word. The psychographer medium, surrendering hand, mind, neutrality, allows the spirit to communicate directly with the physical plane through written language. And when this spirit is a protective guide, an elevated mentor, or even a collective intelligence linked to light, the words transform into invisible shields.

In Kardecist Spiritism, codified by Allan Kardec in the 19th century, psychography holds a central place. Entire works were received through it, like Chico Xavier's books—who acted not as author, but instrument. But far beyond books or messages for third parties, exists a less explored yet extremely powerful branch: defensive psychography. The kind seeking not just teaching, but diagnosing, revealing subtle attacks, protecting the medium's own field.

Defensive psychography acts as a mirror. When well-practiced, it reveals hidden patterns of spiritual obsession, negative influences, extraphysical pressures, open breaches. Sessions where the medium writes words pointing to specific interferences are not rare: names of obsessing spirits, unresolved emotional causes, unconscious vibrational contracts, karmic cycles yet untranscended. Facing such information, the practitioner is no longer blind—they see, and what is seen begins to dissolve.

For psychography to have this protective effect, however, preparation is needed. The medium's field must be clean. The environment neutral, protected, sealed. Before starting practice, lighting a white candle, offering sincere prayer, using light smudging, and invoking familiar spiritual guides is recommended. The pen should be simple, paper white, posture comfortable. Silence cultivated. Writing is not forced—it should flow.

Psychography can manifest in various forms. Sometimes with altered handwriting. Others, with words the medium doesn't know. It might appear as short phrases, entire pages, symbolic drawings, simple loose words. What matters is not aesthetics—but vibration. And this vibration can be felt in the body. True psychography leaves the field lighter, more lucid, cohesive. Even when revealing difficult truths, there is a sense of liberation.

At the end of each session, reading what was written with presence is recommended. Read softly, as if a prayer. Some words have sounds activating codes in the subtle field. Others are like decrees. And there are texts that must be burned, buried, or torn after reading, according to received guidance. Because psychography is also ritual. And every ritual has a sacred end.

Besides individual protection, defensive psychography can protect environments. Psychographing specific guidance for a house, room, spiritual temple, the medium receives directions about objects to remove, points to seal, crystals to position, symbols to draw. These messages come not from conscious mind—but from subtle reading by guides of the location's energy field.

In well-structured spiritual houses, psychography is used as a screening tool. A medium with a trained field can receive messages even before a mediumistic session begins, revealing types of entities that will manifest, vibrational traps prepared for that day, weak points of the group. With this, protections can be reinforced, work reconfigured, serious spiritual accidents prevented.

But there are dangers. Psychography without guidance can become an entry point for mystifying spirits, sophisticated obsessors, or the medium's own mental fragments. This occurs especially with inflated ego, desire for control, anxiety for answers, or empty curiosity. An impure medium attracts impure words.

And what seems a sacred message might actually be subtle manipulation. Therefore, practitioner discernment is essential.

Discernment arises from frequency. True guides bring peace. Dense, angry, critical words generating fear or exaltation should be questioned. Light never attacks. The elevated spirit does not threaten, boast, impose. It guides, reveals, liberates. And if the psychographed message generates heaviness, restlessness, doubt, it should be set aside, awaiting confirmation. No word, however beautiful, is worth more than the vibration with which it was received.

Many mediums begin their spiritual process awakening precisely through writing. Dreams with messages, phrases emerging during meditation, feelings that "someone is dictating." These are common signs the psychography field is activating. Ignoring this call can cause imbalance—as energy accumulates. Heeding it, with humility and guidance, can open extraordinary doors for spiritual service and self-protection.

It's important to remember psychography is not an exclusive gift. It is a trainable skill. The more the practitioner cleanses their field, silences their mind, cultivates their bond with guides, the clearer the channel becomes. It is not about spectacular mediumship—but attunement. And attunement results from vibrational affinity. Therefore, practice often takes time to consolidate. Each writing is a step. Each silence, preparation.

In traditions like Theosophy, psychography is seen as expression of the higher soul. Madame

Blavatsky, Rudolf Steiner, other masters wrote entire works under influence of higher consciousnesses, not as unconscious mediumship, but states of superconsciousness. In these cases, the lower self silences, the higher self dictates. The protection generated by this type of writing is profound—it reorganizes the planet's own field.

But even in simple, domestic, discreet practices, writing from light generates shield. Psychography can also seal objects. Writing a mantra, divine name, channeled sacred code on paper and placing inside an amulet, crystal, bottle with herbs, creates a vibrational talisman. The written word, in this case, acts as anchor for intention. The paper, though fragile, becomes repository of programmed energy. And where this word is, light pulses.

Finally, understand that defensive psychography is not just writing—it is prayer in trace form. Each letter traced truthfully becomes a line of light. Each word captured silently becomes an invisible wall. Each message received humbly becomes a sharp blade against deception. The medium writing not only channels—arms their spirit with consciousness.

In its purest form, defensive psychography is an alliance between worlds. A silent pact between medium and subtle planes, where the act of writing transforms into a rite of listening. The hand tracing letters is, above all, an ear that learned to silence ego to hear the soul—and beyond it, those watching over its journey. This practice, when mature, serves not just clarifying personal dilemmas or punctual protection. It becomes a path of deep self-knowledge, where each received message refines perception of the invisible and strengthens the practitioner's spiritual integrity. Like a sword made of word, psychography protects not only by revealing, but by aligning the being with what is true.

Developing on this path, the medium also confronts responsibility for what they write. It is tempting to yield to fascination with beautiful or impactful messages, but true commitment lies with vibrational coherence. Psychographing requires constant vigilance—over one's own field, intentions, inner silences. And the more this channel purifies, the more reliable it becomes not only for oneself, but also for serving others.

There are cases where messages psychographed in moments of deep connection act as spiritual seals remaining active for years, protecting people, places, entire lineages. Because the word, when born from light, is alive—and continues vibrating long after the instant it was written. Defensive psychography, therefore, is more than mediumistic gift—it is spiritual art. A practice uniting surrender, technique, discernment, love. Writing truthfully, the medium arms themselves with their own lucidity, seals their field with knowledge, walks in alliance with higher planes. And in this simple gesture, of surrendering the hand to what is unseen, lies one of the oldest, most effective forms of spiritual protection: the word from light, written on paper and in spirit.

Chapter 25
Tai Chi and Vital Energy

There is a force traversing everything. Invisible, subtle, present in the air breathed, blood flow, wind's breath, stars' dance. It is called Qi, Chi, Prana, Vital Force. Many names for the same essence animating the universe and human being. When this energy flows freely, there is health, clarity, protection. When stagnant, illness, confusion, spiritual vulnerability. Tai Chi Chuan, ancient Chinese art, was born from studying this energy. And when practiced consciously, transforms into a true shield against forces draining the spirit.

Tai Chi is not fighting, though it has martial roots. Nor dance, though its movements are beautiful and fluid. It is meditation in motion, bodily alchemy, rite of integration between heaven and earth. Each gesture, step, transition is a symbol. And these symbols are aimed not at spectacle, but internal reorganization. The practitioner does not "do" Tai Chi—they become the circulating energy itself, spiraling between worlds.

In Taoist tradition, the body is a temple traversed by meridians, invisible channels where Qi circulates. These meridians connect organs, emotions, thoughts, spirit. When the practitioner performs Tai Chi movements, they are unblocking these channels, allowing life's flow to run fully again. Simultaneously, sealing subtle openings through which attacks, vampirism, destructive thought-forms entered.

Each Tai Chi form—Chen, Yang, Wu, Sun—has its own characteristic. Some more explosive, others gentler. But all share the same purpose: restoring the body's natural axis. Continuous practice strengthens the center—known as dantian—the reservoir of vital energy below the navel. When this center is active and expanded, the entire body illuminates from within. The vibrational field becomes cohesive. And the being begins vibrating at a frequency naturally repelling all dissonant.

Posture is essential. In Tai Chi, nothing is accidental. Aligning spine with earth and sky is not just aesthetics—it is channeling. Earth energy rises through feet. Celestial energy descends through crown. The practitioner, maintaining posture with dignity and relaxation, becomes bridge. And this bridge is naturally protected. Because where Qi flows abundantly, shadow finds no foothold.

Tai Chi's circular, spiraling, continuous, gentle movements directly affect the auric field. They reorganize aura layers, seal breaches, undo knots. It is as if the body redraws its field with invisible ink. Many practitioners report sensations of tingling, heat, inner wind, lightness after practice. These sensations indicate flow was restored. Vital energy, once trapped, now dances.

Breathing is another Tai Chi pillar. Not breathing mechanically, but cultivating breath with presence. Inhaling from the root, guiding air to center, exhaling consciously. Tai Chi breathing nourishes not just lungs—but spirit. Over time, mind quiets, nervous system balances, practitioner recognizes early signs of spiritual attack more easily. Body warns. Breath alters. Tai Chi offers remedy in movement form.

In ancient times, Taoist monks used Tai Chi not just for longevity, but spiritual defense. They knew moving the body attuned to elements—water, fire, earth, metal, wood—invoked cyclical harmony. And where harmony exists, no room for imbalance. During protection ceremonies, masters used specific movements to seal temples, purify environments, reorganize invisible battlefields.

Tai Chi also acts emotionally. Anger, fear, guilt, sadness are condensed energy forms. When not flowing, become portals. Portals for obsessors, astral parasites, dense influences. Continuous practice dissolves these emotions in movement. Practitioner does not repress—moves. Moving, releases. Releasing, protects. Emotion not stagnating does not become breach.

Many confuse spiritual protection with resistance. But Tai Chi teaches the strongest is not he who resists, but he who flows. Water does not break—contours. Wind does not fight—traverses. The body trained in Tai Chi learns absorbing impact, returning it transformed. This wisdom extends to subtle plane. A spiritual attack need not be fought with energetic violence. Can be welcomed, dissolved, returned as light.

Compared to yoga, Tai Chi is more fluid, less static. While yoga works with postures, sustenance, Tai Chi works with transition, continuity. Both complement.

Tai Chi practice prepares field for deep meditation. Stabilizes chakras, purifies channels, anchors presence. An anchored mind is greatest shield.

Compared to Reiki, Tai Chi is more bodily. Reiki channels energy with hands. Tai Chi generates energy with entire body. But both deal with same essence: Qi. Integrating both is potent. A Reiki practitioner also practicing Tai Chi expands channeling capacity. A meditator incorporating Tai Chi strengthens aura. A magician learning Tai Chi principles discovers moving magic circle forces with entire body.

In Tai Chi, external movement always reflects internal. Visible gesture expresses invisible. When arm lifts, intention raises it. When leg shifts, spirit guides it. Each sequence—called form—is like poem in action. Each poem, bodily mantra. Recited with muscles, breath, soul.

For those wishing to use Tai Chi as spiritual protection practice, establishing daily ritual is ideal. At dawn, before world starts shouting, body stands, breathes, moves intentionally. Mind calms. Field organizes. Day then begins with shield activated. Even if world's chaos tries penetrating, finds cohesive field. Because Qi already anchored.

What if attack is intense? Negativity dense? Movements like "Repulse Monkey," "Grasp Sparrow's Tail," "Pulling Silk" dissipate density. Gestures of deflection, transmutation, return to center. Evil not faced with force. Faced with axis. Tai Chi teaches being like bamboo: flexible, yet unbreakable.

This silent wisdom of Tai Chi—teaching dancing with energy instead of resisting it—awakens finer perception of what being protected truly means. Not creating rigid barriers or living constantly alert, but cultivating an energy field so integral and harmonized it becomes naturally inaccessible to dissonant frequencies. Practitioner need not react to attack, because already out of reach. This state results from gentle discipline, constant presence, body moving as channel, spirit anchored in flow. And this stability, more than any amulet or power word, is true shield.

Furthermore, Tai Chi reintegrates being with universe intelligence. Repeating ancient gestures evoking five elements, practitioner reactivates balance archetypes inscribed not just physically, but in humanity's collective field. Practice then becomes more than personal—aligns with ancestral flow sustaining life's harmony. Moving arms like crane's flight or turning torso like water's movement, body relearns nature's original language. And where this language is spoken, no room for imbalance. Field becomes sacred landscape, living, self-adjusting.

Thus, understanding Tai Chi as spiritual protection instrument means recognizing true strength lies not in rigidity, but conscious fluidity. Not attack gesture protecting, but gesture returning to center. And in this center, where heaven meets earth, body aligns with soul, no shadow remains long. Tai Chi practitioner seeks not defending—learns vibrating so integrally that presence itself is protection.

Chapter 26
Symbolic Sacrifices

Since the times when humans still walked barefoot on sacred earth and looked to the heavens for answers, sacrifice presented itself as a bridge between worlds. Not as gratuitous pain, but as a vibrational language communicating a decision, a surrender, a renunciation to the invisible. Sacrifice, in its deepest essence, is not destruction—it is transmutation. And when understood symbolically, it becomes one of the most refined forms of spiritual protection.

The act of offering something one possesses in the name of a higher intention traverses cultures, continents, and religions. In ancient Judaism, lambs and doves were sacrificed as a form of redemption. In Vedic Hinduism, offerings of milk, fruits, and ghee were cast into the sacred fire in honor of the devas. In Candomblé, foods are prepared with ritualistic precision and offered to the orishas, in a sacred dance between the visible and the invisible. But in all these practices, what matters is not the object—it is the vibration with which it is offered.

In Candomblé and Umbanda, symbolic sacrifice takes deep ritual forms. When food is offered at the foot of a tree, when a candle is lit at a crossroads, when honey is poured over a stone, one is not just performing an external gesture. One is signing a vibrational pact with a spiritual force. The food, perfume, smoke, oil become messengers between planes. And these offerings, made ethically and consciously, function as energetic payment for protection, healing, direction.

In Judaism, the Kaparot ritual is a living example of symbolic transmutation. During the Yom Kippur period, the energy of potential misdeeds is symbolically transferred to a white chicken, which is then donated to poor families after the rite. In more modern communities, the chicken is replaced by money or bread. The ritual's essence remains: giving something of oneself to cleanse the field, relieve the soul, and realign with the divine. What is given becomes a shield.

In Christianity, the greatest symbol of sacrifice is Christ himself. His surrendered body, his shed blood, become eternal archetypes of a surrender surpassing flesh. In the rite of the Eucharist, bread and wine represent this sacrifice perpetuated in every mass. But more than religious symbols, they are portals of spiritual activation. He who participates in this rite consciously, offering himself as an instrument of peace, accesses a field of protection transcending centuries.

Nowadays, symbolic sacrifice takes subtler forms. Fasts, vows of silence, abstinence from pleasures, renunciation of harmful patterns—all these are modern sacrifices. They do not bleed the body but discipline the soul. A vow of silence during a lunar cycle, for example, can become shielding against spiritual attacks. A fast from negative words for seven days cleanses the vibrational field with the force of a subtle exorcism. A conscious renunciation of an addiction, a toxic relationship, a destructive behavior activates changes in the field reverberating throughout the entire spiritual network connected to the individual.

In Islam, the sacrifice of a lamb during Eid al-Adha is not an act of cruelty, but remembrance. It remembers the story of Abraham, willing to offer his most precious possession. The meat is divided among family, neighbors, and the needy. The offering is made not to the divine out of vanity, but as recognition of a greater force. Today, many Muslims replace the animal with donations, social actions, or symbolic offerings. The essence remains: give to protect. Release to receive.

In shamanism, sacrifice is made not with blood, but presence. Offering leaves, tobacco, crystals, pieces of bread, or even strands of hair to nature's elements is not random. Each element carries a part of the practitioner. And when offered to earth, fire, river, or wind, communicates to the place's spirit that there is respect, intention, truth. In return, the territory opens, the portal aligns, protection is established.

But there are dangers. Sacrifice, when made without clarity, ethics, or with distorted intention, transforms into a pact of imbalance. The universe responds to the gesture with the same vibration it was made with. A sacrifice for vengeance attracts war. A sacrifice for vanity attracts illusion. A sacrifice without heart is just theater. Therefore, every symbolic gesture must be preceded by introspection, honesty, discernment.

In the field of magic, symbolic sacrifice is part of the so-called "principle of exchange." Something is offered in the name of something greater. But this exchange should not be seen as commerce. It is alliance. It is telling the invisible: "I am willing to transform myself." Many magicians offer their hours, sleep, rituals, disciplines as offerings. And the field responds. Because the most powerful sacrifice is not made with hands, but with time.

Discipline, for example, is a type of continuous sacrifice. Rising always at the same time to pray. Practicing meditation even when the mind screams. Keeping the altar clean. Completing a practice cycle rigorously. These small daily renunciations, when made consciously, become invisible armor. Each day fulfilled strengthens the field. Each gesture maintained generates a wave. And this wave, over time, transforms into lasting protection.

In Kabbalistic practice, sacrifices are subtle but profound. Studying divine names daily, writing psalms, offering specific prayers on sacred days—all require time, focus, surrender. The soul fulfilling these practices is renouncing ego, mundane time, noise. And every second offered to the divine, without expecting immediate return, is a seed of protection. Kabbalah teaches that everything done in the name of light, truthfully, returns multiplied. Including the shield.

For symbolic sacrifice to become real protection, three elements must be present: intention, surrender, silence. Intention aligns gesture with spirit. Surrender transforms act into truth. Silence prevents ego from stealing the action's merit. The spoken, boasted, spread offering loses part of its strength. Because true protection arises in the invisible. And the invisible responds best to silence.

When the sacrificial gesture is imbued with pure, silent intention, it ceases to be a mere ceremonial act and operates as spiritual technology. In this space, where materiality yields to symbolic language, each offering acts as a key unlocking subtle realities. It is the space where the invisible is summoned not by spectacle's force, but by the legitimate vibration of the offerer. And the more discreet this surrender, the more profoundly it acts, for in many traditions, what is hidden preserves its potency. This is the invisible ethic of the sacred: what is done truthfully, even if unseen, is recorded in the spirit's weavings.

There is also a raw beauty in understanding that symbolic sacrifice serves not only to protect us from the external world, but primarily to protect us from ourselves. From the parts that sabotage, repeat harmful patterns, cling to illusions. Renouncing these parts, day after day, is an act of spiritual courage. Instead of waiting for an external miracle, the practitioner transforms into a living altar, a conscious offering, a messenger between planes. And this process requires more than faith: it requires constancy, presence, and a surrender that does not justify itself, merely realizes itself.

Thus, symbolic sacrifice fulfills its noblest role—not pleasing deities, but reminding the soul who it is and where it is returning. When performed truthfully, symbolic sacrifice needs no audience, nor others' understanding. It suffices in itself, because it touches a frequency where time doesn't matter and space bends. It is in this ritualistic silence that protection rises like an invisible wall, aligning worlds and steadying the soul on its journey. By transforming daily gestures into offerings, the practitioner not only defends—they consecrate themselves.

Chapter 27
Spiritual Cyberprotection

Nowadays, the spiritual world no longer resides only in ancestral forests, consecrated *terreiros*, or silent temples. It also traverses invisible cables, pulses in data waves, breathes through screens. The digital is not just technology—it is environment. And like any environment, it carries field, frequencies, intentions, presences. There are spirits manifesting in typed words, obsessors vibrating in memes, thought-forms fixing on social networks. Protecting oneself spiritually, in this new era, requires adapting old practices to the soul's new abode: cyberspace.

Spiritual cyberprotection is the art of preserving energetic integrity amidst digital exposure. It involves recognizing that accessing a virtual environment expands and interacts with the vibrational field. There is no separation between mind and network. Each post, message, comment is a connecting thread—carrying energy. Just as a house is cleaned, an altar sealed, or a body purified, the vibration of cell phones, computers, virtual accounts, and online interactions also needs care.

The first practice of cyberprotection is recognizing the digital field as an extension of the spiritual body. The social media profile is not just image—it is energetic avatar. When someone sends a message with anger, envy, malice, that energy vibrates in the recipient's field. Even if deleted, the frequency remains if not purified. Similarly, a post made in pain or confusion can become an attraction point for invisible obsessors inhabiting the internet's collective emotional fields.

Excessive exposure of intimate life, for example, creates breaches. Sharing high emotional charge images—births, achievements, relationships—without grounding opens the field to subtle vampirism. Often, energy drops, sudden conflicts, or abrupt illnesses after published "good news" have spiritual origins. They are forms of invisible interference using the digital channel as vector.

Therefore, one of the simplest, most effective practices is vibrational programming of electronic devices. Before turning on the cell phone, the practitioner can place hands over it for seconds, visualizing a sphere of blue or golden light enveloping the device. This visualization, repeated daily, creates a vibrational layer filtering incoming energies. The same technique applies to computers, associating the gesture with invoking mental field protection: "May everything coming through this screen be filtered by the light of consciousness."

Another powerful resource is using protection sigils adapted to the virtual environment. The practitioner can draw a personal symbol—formed by letters, numbers, geometric shapes—representing security, lucidity, shielding. This symbol can be digitized and used as wallpaper, profile picture, or printed and glued to devices' backs. These sigils function as conscious anchors, programmed to keep the field clean.

Passwords can also carry spiritual function. Creating passwords for email, social media, any system, the practitioner can include numerological codes or embedded sacred words. Sequences like 777, guides' names, power words like "Shalom," "Om," "Lux," when inserted intentionally, become invisible seals vibrating each time typed. Each access becomes a micro ritual activating the field.

Energetic cleansing of devices should be periodic. Deleting messages or uninstalling apps isn't enough. Purification is needed. A simple method is passing smoke from sage, rosemary, or myrrh incense around devices, like digital smudging. During the process, mentally repeat a cleansing invocation, like: "May all dense energy be transmuted into light. May this digital channel be consecrated to truth, good, protection." Using sounds—Tibetan bowls, mantras, 528 Hz frequency music played near the device—also helps reorganize its vibrational field.

Another layer of cyberprotection involves care with consumed content. Aggressive videos, sensationalist news, polarized discussions, violent images—all are spiritual food. And like all food, generate residue. Social media algorithms understand not light nor shadow—understand repetition. The more dense content accessed, the more offered. Thus the field drowns in patterns of fear, anger, judgment. Spiritual protection, in this context, requires fasting. Digital detox. Sacred pauses. Moments of electronic silence.

Some practice digital sabbath, inspired by Jewish traditions' rest days. One day per week without screens. No connection. Just presence. During this day, field reorganizes, mind rests, spirit breathes. Others prefer "dead hours"—programmed periods daily when all devices are off, light softened, connection turned inward. These practices, though simple, become living shields amidst the subtle bombardment of the digital world.

Cyberprotection also involves vigilance over conversations and virtual groups. Constant message exchanges with unbalanced people, groups full of gossip, low-vibration jokes, toxic discussions generate energetic threads between participants. Even when the phone is far, these connections remain active on the astral plane. The sensitive practitioner notices: restless sleep, intrusive thoughts, focus loss. In these cases, cutting these threads is essential. This can be done with a small ritual: write group/people names on paper, burn with sage or bay leaf, declare: "I now cut all invisible ties draining my energy. I free myself and release."

Spiritual cyberprotection is, therefore, vibrational vigilance. Recognizing spiritual warfare happens not just in cemeteries, power centers, astral planes—also present in post comments, silent heavy messages, videos simulating joy but carrying despair. And the practitioner, awakening to this, learns navigating with shield.

Digital prayers are also possible. Some create specific device folders with sacred audios, protection images, channeled texts. Others program phones to play mantras at dawn/dusk, times traditionally linked to spiritual portal changes. Some leave open documents with psalms/prayers, using as first reading when opening computer. Each gesture, however small, emits decree: "This channel belongs to light."

For practitioners of mediumship or heightened sensitivity, greater care is needed with videos of rituals, incorporation, recorded magic practices. Watching, even unintentionally, opens channel. Often, recording's field still carries fragments of original ritual. Absorption is real. Thus, viewings only at specific times, with active protection, preferably with clear learning intention—never curiosity.

Understanding the digital world as spiritual territory, the practitioner ceases being mere user, becomes guardian. Cultivates online presence like altar. Just as no one allows sacred temple profanation, neither allows profile, device, typed words become breaches. Everything consecrated. Everything cared for.

Because in the end, evil needs no physical body to enter. Enters through carelessness. Unconscious exposure. Repetition without vigil. And light, when awakened digitally, is as powerful as in ancestral rituals. Spreads through cables, signals, frequencies. Where it vibrates, no virus remains. Neither digital, nor astral.

This new paradigm demands, therefore, active, adaptive spirituality, where consciousness becomes main antivirus. He who transits cyberspace lucidly understands each click can be pact, each like, invocation, each share, mirroring. Nothing neutral regarding energy. Thus, more than creating protection barriers, involves cultivating continuous presence. Like digital monk, practitioner observes each online gesture, understanding spirituality is not where one is, but how one vibrates—even before screen.

This vigilance, however, translates not into paranoia, but reverence. Cyberspace, when consecrated, can become healing tool, bridge for elevated encounters, space for collective prayer. Online meditation groups, sacred ritual broadcasts, conscious sharing—all signs light also found place online. Spiritual protection then expands beyond defense: becomes architecture. A way building subtle dwellings within data network, where soul feels safe expressing, learning, serving, growing. Each conscious gesture becomes brick in this invisible temple rising amidst Wi-Fi.

In the end, spiritual cyberprotection isn't appendix to spiritual practice—its inevitable continuation. Because as long as connection exists, flow exists. As long as flow exists, exchange exists. New era challenge not denying technology, but consecrating it. Not fearing digital dangers, but making it mirror internal light. When spirit manifests also in codes, invisible becomes present in cables. And in this new virtual altar, conscious presence becomes greatest firewall existing.

Chapter 28
Ecology and Planetary Defense

There is a truth many refuse to see: the Earth is also a spiritual body. It breathes, pulses, feels. Beneath oceans and mountains, among forests and winds, an invisible heart beats silently. They call it Gaia, Pachamama, Great Mother, Living Body of Creation. And when she sickens, all inhabiting her sicken together. Protecting oneself spiritually, in today's world, also means protecting the planet. Not out of ideology, but connection. Because Earth's soul is mother to ours.

Ecology, understood through a spiritual lens, reveals itself as sacred practice. More than environmental science, it is life's liturgy. Each act of care—planting a tree, cleaning a river, recycling waste, consuming consciously—becomes an act of collective spiritual defense. Because there is no separation between the human vibrational field and Earth's field. All environmental destruction creates an energetic fissure. And through these fissures enter dense entities, unbalanced forces, shadows feeding on chaos generated by disconnection.

Ancient traditions knew this. Indigenous peoples, shamans, druids, ancient priests—all maintained rituals connecting with Earth not just as thanksgiving, but spiritual balance. At each equinox, solstice, full moon, ceremonies were performed not to ask, but give. Symbolic offerings, chants, circle dances, smudging, fasts, night vigils. Earth revered as spirit. And this reverence became protection.

In shamanic tradition, Earth is the first altar. Before connecting with any higher force, practitioner must be grounded. "Grounding" is more than metaphor—it's technique. Sitting directly on soil, barefoot, spine erect, breathing deeply, visualizing roots extending from feet towards Earth's center, creates stability field blocking obsessions, psychic imbalances. Because where connection with Gaia exists, shield exists.

In Andean cultures, Pachamama is honored with offerings called "mesas." Small arrangements containing coca leaves, flowers, grains, sweets, fabrics, all arranged with symbolic precision. These mesas are buried or burned in specific ceremonies. The gesture is not folkloric—it's magical. Rebalances practitioner's energy field with planet's field. Doing so seals invisible protection acting on subtlest planes.

In the New Age view, Gaia is cosmic consciousness choosing to inhabit matter. Considered evolving planetary entity, connected to interdimensional network of living planets. According to this perspective, each ecological action affects not just physical planet, but reverberates in other dimensions. Depolluting river, for example, cleanses energetic channel potentially crossing planes. Reforesting damaged area is like healing wound on Earth's subtle body. And this process, done with spiritual consciousness, generates protection not just for practitioner, but humanity's entire collective grid.

Apometry, Brazilian spiritual practice uniting mediumship with vibrational science, recognizes Earth as multidimensional energy field. In many works, practitioners act on planet's astral layers, reprogramming memories of war, violence, environmental destruction. In these actions, Earth treated as spiritual patient. Cleansing planetary fields prevents dense consciousnesses grouping, strengthening harmful egregore. Participating in such works strengthens practitioner's own field, becoming part of collective healing.

Planetary defense rituals can be done individually. Walking trail collecting trash, each removed object repeated mentally: "I cleanse, I heal, I seal." Lighting green candle over Earth map, chanting mantras or planetary healing prayers. Meditating visualizing Earth enveloped in golden light network, healing points lighting where pain exists. Each gesture, however small, acts on field. Because field responds to intention.

There are also global prayer networks, formed by groups meditating, praying for planet at specific times. These groups create what's called "coherent field"—unified vibrational frequency reverberating beyond time, space. Scientific studies, like those by HeartMath Institute, proved groups in cardiac coherence can affect surrounding chaos patterns. Applied spiritually, this practice becomes shield. Where light network exists, shadow doesn't settle.

Spiritual ecology also invites conscious consumption practices. Avoiding products generating suffering, reducing plastic use, preferring local, seasonal foods, all form vibrational pattern sustaining harmony between body, planet. Practitioner eating respecting Earth generates cleaner field. This field doesn't attract obsessors. Because ethical vibration repels disharmonious.

In times of environmental collapse, each ecological gesture is also magical act. Composting becomes offering. Planting becomes prayer. Animal care transforms into invocation of balance. River cleaning becomes exorcism. Ecological activism, guided by spirit, ceases being just political—becomes liturgical.

But detail: planetary defense isn't fanaticism. Doesn't demand perfection. Isn't about guilt. About alignment. Recognizing that caring for Earth means caring for own soul. Remembering human body made of same clay, water, breath. Breathing, shares air with trees. Sleeping, rests on Mother's womb.

Earth responds. Some hear her. In dreams, she speaks. In winds, whispers. In earthquakes, screams. But above all, welcomes. Even wounded, exploited, ignored, continues offering food, shelter, beauty. Protecting oneself spiritually, now, means giving back. Returning consciousness Earth offers us.

In the end, understanding ecology as spiritual protection means recognizing no individual salvation. All healing collective. Personal field only shielded when planet's vibration rises. This begins with each gesture.

Each choice. Each silence before sunset. Each barefoot step on wet earth.

This understanding transforms the practitioner into a guardian—not just of self, but of a sacred ecosystem where everything vibrates in network. Spirituality recognizing Earth as living being transcends isolated practices, becomes way of life. Listening to nature ceases being metaphor, becomes daily practice: feeling soil, dialoguing with plants, interpreting signs of wind, cycles, animals. In this state of presence, spiritual protection merges with reverence. And this reverence shapes choices: how one eats, discards, occupies space, gives thanks upon receiving. Nothing neutral. Each interaction with natural world is energetic exchange—every conscious exchange becomes shield.

Thus, protecting Earth becomes act of expanded self-defense. Because when soil heals, surroundings' frequency changes. When animal saved, collective emotional field elevates. When planting with love, seeds' vibrational network expands. These small actions activate silent circuit protecting, consoling, strengthening.

In times of psychic exhaustion, global energetic instability, connecting with Earth one of few true remedies. Spiritual sensitivity no longer luxury—necessity. And planet, with millennial patience, still offers itself as open temple to those willing to feel.

In the end, planetary defense is practice of remembrance. Remembering we are nature. Not living *on* Earth, but *with* her. That each being—stone, cloud, tree, serpent—participates in invisible choir intoning creation's song. Protecting this song protects sacred name inhabiting us. Because spirituality rooted in ecology returns practitioner to original function: bridge between Heaven, Earth. And no bridge stands if unaware of banks supporting it.

Chapter 29
Oaths and Pacts

There are words that seal destinies. Vows traversing time. Commitments not undone by forgetting, nor broken by death. They vibrate, persist, mark the spiritual field like invisible inscriptions on the soul's flesh. They are oaths and pacts—sacred alliances, silent, sometimes forgotten, but never annulled without due rite. And when understood in depth, become powerful instruments of spiritual protection, provided they are established with lucidity, ethics, truth.

An oath is more than promise. It is vibrational decree. Pronounced with intention, emotion, shapes individual's subtle field, links energy to specific force, establishes flow channel between being, what is sworn. Vow of silence, for example, not just absence of words—activation of internal listening channel, field repelling noise, protecting against external influence. Vow of chastity, when true, not repression—containment of creative energy, transforming into protective light.

In Buddhist traditions, especially Mahayana, Vajrayana schools, vows essential part of spiritual journey. Practitioner starts with lay precepts—not killing, stealing, lying—deepening, enters bodhisattva vows—committing to liberate all beings from suffering. Such vows not symbolic. Shape destiny, create shields. Bodhisattva not attacked because intention protects. Light of promise, sealed with heart, envelops like invisible breastplate.

In mystical Kabbalah, pacts made with Divine Names. Student committing daily recitation certain Hebrew names—like YHVH, El Shaddai, Adonai—creates direct channel with creation's archetypal forces. These forces, evoked purely, create vibrational seals repelling dense entities, dissolving curses, strengthening invoker's field. But name not recited vainly. Requires preparation, reverence, surrender. Because where divine pact exists, field demands continuous alignment.

Among indigenous, shamanic peoples, pacts often silent, transmitted by rite, not speech. Apprentice receiving tobacco breath from master, watching forest at night unfearing spirits, dancing around fire fasting deeply, establishes commitments with elementals, ancestors, nature's invisible forces. These pacts need no contract. Soul recognizes what sealed.

But there are also oaths made in past lives, continuing operating even when conscious ignores them. Poverty vow by monk in another existence manifests today as financial blockage. Celibacy vow by priestess prevents deep relationships now. Oath protecting someone with own life attracts constant sacrifice situations. These ancient pacts, when unrevoked or updated, act as auric field codes, creating repetitive patterns.

Conscious revocation of outdated vows, pacts important spiritual practice. Can be done through simple, intense rituals. One involves writing what intuited sworn—even uncertainly—on paper. Beside it, write new choice. Example: "I now revoke, in name of light inhabiting me, any vow of silence, suffering, servitude made in past lives. I now assume my right to freedom, expression, joy." Paper then burned with purification herbs—like sage, rue, bay leaf. Ashes blown to wind or offered to earth.

Pacts with entities also require attention. In some Afro-Brazilian traditions, like Umbanda, Quimbanda, pacts made with Exu, Pomba Gira, other path guardians. These pacts not demonic—ethical contracts between human, spiritual. Medium offers something—dedication, silence, practice—receives protection, path opening, guidance. But rules exist. Disrespected pact becomes vulnerability point. Not punishment, but vibrational deviation.

In ceremonial magic universe, pacts recorded precisely. Evocations of planetary intelligences, invocations of archangels, seals traced intentionally, names engraved on candles, crystals, consecrated papers—all constitute vibrational contract. He who pacts with force must know it. Because where unconscious pact exists, risk exists. True spiritual protection born from knowledge. Sealing field with unknown symbols like signing contract unread.

There are also soul pacts between people. Relationships repeating over lifetimes. Promises made on deathbed. Alliances sealed in wartime. These pacts often appear as inexplicable connections, loves defying logic, unbreakable bonds. Some protect, others imprison. When soul pact fulfilled function, must be released with love. Simple energetic cutting ritual done with two candles—one per soul—linked by thread. After prayer, clear release intention, thread cut. Flame remains—prison dissolves.

Practitioner wishing firm sacred pact for own protection can do with four elements. On simple altar, position candle (fire), glass water (water), incense/herb (air), crystal/stone (earth). In state of presence, declare: "In name of light inhabiting me, forces guiding me, I now establish pact with my truth. Commit watching over integrity, listening intuition, respecting cycles, walking clearly. May this pact protect me, remind me who I am." Then extinguish candle, drink water, blow incense, keep crystal as seal.

Oaths can also be renewed cyclically. Each new moon, for example, recommit to own soul. No need grand rituals. Simple act sitting silently, hand over heart, reaffirming: "I remain faithful to my light," emits protection code. Universe listens what said truthfully.

But every oath requires vigilance. Words are seeds. Promising what cannot be fulfilled signs contracts with chaos. Spirituality respects free will—field doesn't forget what said emotionally. Protection also born from wise silence. Sometimes, not pact-making purest protection form.

Spiritual maturity reveals itself largely in how these invisible alliances are handled. Conscious practitioner swears not impulsively, pacts not desperately. Understands each word emitted in elevated emotional state opens portals, moves forces, binds destinies. Therefore, before sealing any vibrational commitment, consults silence, listens body, interrogates soul. Because from internal alignment true pact born—one not imprisoning, but liberating; not demanding, but sustaining; not tying, but guiding. In this dimension, oaths cease being obligations, become luminous paths of self-remembrance.

It is also in this context value of word as magical tool understood. What declared intentionally echoes multi-dimensionally. When practitioner affirms loyalty to light, decrees integrity before invisible, promises no longer denying own essence, not just firming pact with Higher Self—anchoring shields. Fidelity to personal truth becomes spiritual shield. This fidelity requires not grandiosity: manifests in details. Fulfilling self-promises, respecting own cycles, not lying about feelings. Enough for field aligning with protecting forces.

In end, every pact mirror. Reveals not just with whom/what committed, but who chosen be when making it. Spiritual path asks not eternal pacts, but true commitments—with soul, ethics, light dwelling within each. Sometimes, greatest oath possible is not betraying own essence anymore. Because this fidelity, silent, constant, is pact no time undoes.

Chapter 30
Integrated Self-Defense System

Any isolated spiritual protection is a spark. And every spark, however powerful, extinguishes without support. True shield born from convergence. Depends not just on one practice, symbol, belief. Rises as subtle architecture, built precisely, coherently, wisely. Integrated spiritual self-defense system more than set techniques—way of living. Consciousness vibrating in all gestures. Presence sustained each breath.

Soul, by nature, open. Vibrates, pulses, expands. But this openness, uncared for, becomes vulnerable field. External influences—people, places, thoughts, entities—find cracks. Enter. Settle. Often, take place of own will. Thus, first step integrated self-defense system recognizing personal vulnerabilities.

Each being has own form breach. Some open field through fear. Others anger. Some guilt. Others excessive giving. Also those contaminated by dense environments, emotional noise, unsaid words. Recognizing own fragility point act of power. Like discovering exact point shield needs reinforcing. Not fear, but lucidity.

Based on this recognition, protection system designed. Practitioner knowing sensitive to others' emotions might integrate daily grounding practices—

like Tai Chi, herb baths, shield meditation. One overexposing on social media might apply spiritual cyberprotection techniques—sealing devices, cleaning networks, consecrating content. Medium dealing with entities in rituals must maintain living altar—cyclic offerings, specific prayers, personal de-obsession practices.

Secret lies in intelligent composition practices. Not necessary follow all techniques presented throughout work. System personal. But essential it contemplates four anchors: body, mind, field, connection. Body cared for, strengthened, cleaned. Mind watched, silent, ordered. Field shielded, protected, breathing light. Connection alive—with source, guides, purpose.

For body, recommend morning anchor ritual. Can start ingesting consecrated water—water exposed sunlight/moonlight, programmed cleaning intention. Then, conscious breathing practice three minutes, focus on dantian. Next, short sequence body movements—Tai Chi, yoga, simple stretches intentionally. Finish anointing essential oil wrists, nape—lavender psychic protection, rosemary clarity, frankincense spiritual elevation.

Mind needs continuous vibrational hygiene. Includes choosing consumed content, allowed conversations, nourished thoughts. Emotions journal powerful ally—write end day everything felt, unfiltered. Writing, practitioner empties mental field. Where clarity, no breach. Edifying readings, guided meditations, daily spiritual study, even few minutes, keep mind protection frequency.

Subtle field must be cleansed, sealed frequently. Ritualistic baths, smudging, crystal use, applying sacred symbols environments—all compose shielding arsenal. Recommend maintain personal altar, white candle ready lit instability moments. Place coarse salt small containers behind doors, crystals room four corners, mirror facing entrance simple, highly effective measures.

Spiritual connection cultivated like rare flower. Not just praying/asking. Talking with guides, Higher Self, divinity vibrating beyond name. Maintain fixed prayer/meditation time, however brief, daily, seals field. Soul knows heard. Guides know when enter. Regularity creates channel. This channel protection.

Additionally, system consider cyclic spiritual reinforcement moments. Each season change, new moon, birthday, practitioner should remake pacts, renew intentions, cleanse field deeper. Can do one-day silence retreat, technology fast, spiritual vigil. These moments shield recalibrations.

Daily, vigilance great guardian. Felt sudden unexplained fatigue? Pause. Close eyes. Breathe. Touch own chest. Ask: "This energy mine?" If not, release. If is, welcome. Felt strange presence environment? Make seal fingers—sign cross, triskelion, pentagram, per tradition. Repeat mantra. Activate internal symbol. Because shield not something worn—something become.

Crisis moments, have spiritual emergency kit. Coarse salt, white candle, cleansing incense, protection crystal (tourmaline, amethyst, obsidian), small vial holy water/floral essence. Items together, accessible place. Right moment, used intentionally, transform field minutes. Not superstition—preparation.

Integrated self-defense system also requires spiritual ethics. He who harms not protected. He who deceives not shielded. Field responds truth. He manipulating, lying, betraying creates cracks own shield. Path protection also path integrity. Be honest self. Coherent principles. Align thought, word, action. This alone repels evil.

Times great collective spiritual instability, like current, shield must also be communal. Have spiritual friends. Exchange prayers. Care for each other. Mutual protection groups, each watching other's field, strengthen system. Because evil cunning. Attacks where solitude. Where circle, strength.

In end, integrated spiritual self-defense system not made ready formulas. Living organism. Changes time. Evolves soul. Demands not rigidity, but presence. Asks not sacrifice, but constancy. Builds layers. Each practice, choice, chosen silence, becomes stronger.

This path of living protection requires practitioner see self part larger mechanism—being attuned own rhythms, world cycles around. Integrated system not collection disconnected tools, but web practices feeding each other, forming self-defense ecology. Body aligns mind, which pacifies soul, then connects Higher. Thus, shield forms not isolating wall, but field breathing, adapting, expanding, protecting without separating. Presence becomes fortress, daily life, sacred territory.

Precisely because living, system requires listening. Need feel when practice lost strength, symbol no longer resonates, routine needs refinement. Spiritual field responds better authenticity than automatic repetition. Each being unique universe—each system personalized map return own essence. Not copying steps, but recognizing own rhythm. When practitioner understands this, stops seeking external formulas, starts building own protection cartography, based experience, sensitivity, real connection invisible.

In end, protecting self spiritually not fleeing world—learning inhabit world consciously. Walking heart awake, senses aligned, spirit firm light. When self-defense system roots daily practice, silent ethics, applied faith, becomes part being. Then, no matter storm approaching: field remains. Not because shielded everything, but because learned vibrate above noise. This itself highest protection form.

Epilogue

Reaching the end of this work does not signal a conclusion—it marks a passage. A sacred silence settles between the final words and the inner space that opened during this reading. Because everything revealed here asks not just for understanding, but integration. And whoever has reached this point is no longer the same person who opened the first page.

Something has already reorganized in your field, even if subtly. The invisible, now named, recognized, and respected, becomes a living part of your consciousness.

You have journeyed a path traversing millennia, traditions, and dimensions. You walked alongside invisible elders, guardians of light, symbols whispering ancient secrets, words that are more than sounds—they are keys. You explored the vibrational force of intention, the portals contained in mantras, the intelligent fire of smudging, the geometry of the divine in yantras, psalms as walls, and meditation as a silent shield.

Each teaching herein is more than a technique: it is a remembrance. A recollection of what you already knew on some deep level, but which now manifests as active wisdom.

Spiritual protection is not a state of constant defense. It is, in fact, a state of alignment. It is when the human being positions themselves clearly regarding what they allow in and what they decide to keep out. It is when they recognize their home as a temple, their mind as an altar, and their body as a vibrational instrument. By understanding existence as an interactive field of forces, your stance towards life changes: becoming more conscious, selective, lucid.

Nothing said here intends to generate fear. On the contrary: this book is an invitation to sovereignty. To the recognition that the awakened being is not a victim of chance, but a co-creator of their energetic reality. It is not about avoiding the world or fearing shadows, but cultivating light with such intensity that nothing not on the same frequency can remain. This is the true shielding: the vibrational coherence between who one is, what one thinks, what one feels, and what one practices.

And now that the techniques have been offered, symbols presented, and paths outlined, it is you who continues. With tools in hand, but with something even greater: a new perception. The one allowing discernment of when an emotion is yours and when not. When an environment needs cleaning. When a thought arrived uninvited. When a pattern needs breaking. This perception is the beginning of true spiritual freedom.

Constant practice—even if silent—transforms knowledge into presence. Reciting a mantra, lighting an herb, dressing in prayer, sealing an environment with a symbol, building your shield of light at dawn... all this, done with true intention, creates layers of protection that do not fade with the wind. And more than that: it activates an ancestral memory, that you are part of a lineage of beings who always knew how to transit between worlds.

This book, therefore, does not end in itself. It extends into you. Into your choices. Into your ability to transform the everyday into rite, silence into presence, the invisible into ally. Spirituality is not a separate field from life. It is the axis. And when this axis strengthens, life aligns.

Allow yourself to revisit these teachings whenever necessary. There are chapters revealing new layers with each reread, because you will be different each time you return. And living wisdom responds to your level of readiness. Sometimes, just one line reread with a more open heart is enough for a new light to ignite. This work was written as a spiritual organism, pulsing and adapting to the rhythm of who touches it with reverence.

You are now more aware that everything vibrates. That words, thoughts, gestures, spaces are magnetic fields. That intentions shape realities. And that, yes, there are forces testing us—but also forces guarding, elevating, strengthening us. The link with the invisible has been restored. And the responsibility this brings is not burden, but honor.

The spiritual journey has no end. It just changes scenery, depth, intensity. But now, you proceed equipped with discernment. You know how to protect your field, cultivate your light, recognize signs. And, above all, you know ancient wisdoms are available at every step—requiring only silence, presence, intention.

May you walk firmly, humbly, faithfully. May your aura remain clear, your mind vigilant, your soul finally recognized as sacred temple. Because in the end, true protection is born from the center. And the center—that silent point where visible and invisible touch—now pulses within you.

The journey does not end here. It merely reveals itself. And you are ready.

www.ingramcontent.com/pod-product-compliance
Lightning Source LLC
LaVergne TN
LVHW040055080526
838202LV00045B/3650